START AND RUN A PROFITABLE
MAIL ORDER BUSINESS

Your step-by-step business plan

Robert W. Bly

Self-Counsel Press
(a division of)
International Self-Counsel Press Ltd.

Printed in Canada

First edition: May 1997
Reprinted: March 1998

Canadian Cataloguing in Publication Data

    Bly, Robert W.
    Start and run a profitable mail order business

    (Self-counsel series)
    Includes bibliographical references
    ISBN 1-55180-065-9

    1. Mail-order business — Management.   2. Direct marketing.   3. New business
enterprises.   I. Title.   II. Series.
HF5466.B69 1997   658.8'72   C97-910144-1

The Practical Gourmet press release reprinted courtesy of Andrew S. Linick.

Self-Counsel Press
(a division of)
International Self-Counsel Press Ltd.

1481 Charlotte Road   1704 N. State Street
North Vancouver, BC V7J 1H1   Bellingham, WA 98225

To David Yale —
friend, teacher, and colleague

CONTENTS

WORKSHEETS

SAMPLES

ACKNOWLEDGMENTS

Three thank-you's are in order:

First, thanks to my editors, Ruth Wilson, Judy Phillips, Audrey McClellan and to the rest of the crew at Self-Counsel Press. I'm grateful that you chose me to write this book, and I appreciate your help at every step of the way.

Second, thanks to my clients. Writing your mail order space ads, direct mail packages, and sales letters has been a fantastic education in direct marketing. I appreciate your trusting me with your important work.

Third, thanks to my fellow mail order entrepreneurs. By sharing their insight and experience, these friends and colleagues increase my knowledge of the mail order business on a weekly basis. I've also learned a lot from the books and articles they've written. In particular, much of my knowledge comes from reading the works of — and talking with — mail order pros such as Dan Poynter, Jeffrey Lant, Milt Pierce, Andrew Linick, Bob Kalian, Pete Silver, Mark Ford, Paul Karasik, Bill Bonner, Buddy Hayden, Jerry Buchanan, Robert Serling, Bruce Davidson, Neil Raphel, Murray Raphel, Dottie Walters, Joe Vitale, David Yale, and the late Howard Shenson.

Thank you all.

NOTICE TO READERS

INTRODUCTION

Mail order today is a multibillion-dollar industry. More than half of the adults in the United States and Canada buy products through the mail each year. Direct marketing generates annual revenues in North America in excess of $350 billion. More than 50 billion direct mail pieces are mailed annually. These include some 13 billion catalogues (the majority of them, my wife notes, to our home).

The good news for you is that mail order is an ideal entrepreneurial venture . . . one of the few ideal entrepreneurial ventures left in North America today.

What sets mail order apart from most other businesses? It offers high potential profit combined with low start-up costs, and it is flexible. You can do it part time or full time, from a rented office or your home, in your garage, spare bedroom, or even your basement.

There are other advantages to being in the mail order business. You have no boss, no time clock to punch. You need not have direct contact with clients or customers. You can work alone, in peace and tranquillity. Your hours are your own. You don't have to be at a specific place during a specific time. You can live anywhere you want since there's no need to be close to a particular city for commuting to a job.

There is very little rejection in mail order. Learning from experience, yes. Rejection, no. In face-to-face selling, when a salesperson makes a pitch and the customer doesn't want to buy, the customer says "no." This upsets a lot of people and makes them feel bad. In mail order, you don't get rejections; prospects don't write letters or phone to tell you, "I don't want to buy your product!" The only people you hear from, as a rule, are those who want to buy.

Aside from personal and professional service businesses, such as graphic design or word-processing services, mail order is one of the few businesses that can be started for under $500. This compares favorably with the $10,000 to $100,000 required to buy into a successful franchise operation, or the huge investment it takes to start a manufacturing business or open a store or restaurant.

And unlike service businesses, in which your income is restricted by the number of billable hours you can work in a week, the profit potential of a mail order business is virtually unlimited. Some mail order entrepreneurs run their business part time, earning $1,000 to $5,000 or more per month in extra income. Many others have become millionaires, which has allowed them to quit their jobs, stay home, and just open envelopes with checks in them.

This book is aimed at the average reader, the person who wants to start a spare-time mail order business in his or her home with minimal risk and capital. The book will show how to develop a mail order business that generates a handsome second income with virtually no effort and how to expand the business so you can live off the income and quit your job, if that's what you want.

You don't need a college degree or prior business experience. If you can come up with a product people want and find the right way to advertise it, you can be successful in mail order. This book is designed to help you do just that.

I hope the book answers all your questions and gets you started on the road to mail order riches. If it doesn't . . . if you get stuck or have questions or need additional information . . . I'd be happy to help. Also, if you have an ad or mailer that works particularly well, why not send it to me so I can share it with readers of the next edition of this book? You will receive full credit, of course. Simply call or write:

Bob Bly
22 E. Quackenbush Avenue
Dumont, NJ 07628
Phone: (201) 385-1220
Fax: (201) 385-1138
e-mail: Rwbly@aol.com

1
AN OVERVIEW OF THE
MAIL ORDER BUSINESS

a. WHAT IS "MAIL ORDER"?

Mail order has different meanings to different people.

To people who dream of having their own business, mail order is one of the last entrepreneurial ventures the average person can realistically afford to start. If postage rates continue to rise and increasingly complex tax regulations continue to be implemented, it will become more difficult to start a mail order business. But right now it's fairly easy and doesn't require a lot of capital or equipment.

To mail order shoppers, mail order is a great convenience. It eliminates the need to spend time and money driving to malls and fighting the crowds. No more store shopping. Just pick up a catalogue and order items for yourself and gifts for friends and relatives. The mail order companies will even wrap the gifts and deliver them to your mom's front door with a personalized greeting card enclosed.

To those who dislike mail order shopping, mail order is a pain in the neck. Some people resent having their mail boxes stuffed with catalogues, flyers, circulars, and mailers — material they call "junk mail." Although I am a fan of mail order, I understand their feelings. Sometimes there is too much mail in the mail box. On the other hand, I personally find direct mail and magazine ads less intrusive than telemarketing, door-to-door salespeople, and TV and radio commercials. If direct mail and catalogues are "junk mail," commercials are surely "junk TV."

Mail order is a method of selling in which orders are generated, received, and fulfilled remotely, with no face-to-face contact between buyer and seller. Buyers make their purchases sight unseen, buying based on a written description or photograph, or both, rather than hands-on inspection of the product in a store or show room.

The term "mail order" derives from the fact that orders traditionally are received and fulfilled by mail. Although that's still the case, orders are now received through other means, most notably telephone calls (to toll, toll-free, and pay-per-minute 900 numbers), fax, Web sites, and e-mail. Products are still shipped mainly by mail, although a few information products, such as specialized newsletters and business data, are delivered via fax or modem.

Is there really such a thing as the "mail order business"? It depends on your point of view. Consider a company that sells cheese by mail. Some would say the company is in the cheese business, and mail order happens to be the marketing medium it uses to generate sales. Others would say the company is in the mail order business, and that cheese happens to be its main product.

Personally, I do think of myself as being in the mail order business. Mail order has a different feel and flavor than retailing, service, agriculture, construction, manufacturing, and other businesses. It's unique. And I like it better than most other businesses I've been in.

Two things I have noticed about people in the mail order business. First, they seem happy most of the time. They like the business. They enjoy their work. Second, they are free spirits. Most want to control their own time and be in charge of their own destiny. They often don't fit in well as employees working for corporations or organizations. They got into mail order because it is one of the few businesses you can start and run successfully without creating a big organization with a lot of employees and red tape.

b. MY OWN STORY

You bought this book with the hope that I could guide you in the start up and successful launch of your own mail order business. To give you confidence in my advice, please allow me to tell you a little bit about myself and my involvement in mail order. Not to brag — many mail order authorities are orders of magnitude more successful than I — but to give you a feel for the experience and knowledge I have to share with you.

I am not an entrepreneur by nature. I studied chemical engineering in college and worked for several years for various corporations. When my last employer asked me to relocate, I resigned and went into business for myself.

For more than 12 years, I have primarily earned my living as a direct-marketing copywriter and consultant. Mail order companies — small, large, and in-between — hire me to advise them on marketing strategy and to write copy for their ads, brochures, mailings, and catalogues. No doubt you have seen my ads or received mailings written by me. Perhaps I even motivated you to buy my clients' products.

In common with most people in mail order, I find that not everything I do is successful. Some ads and mailers are big winners. Others lose money or are beaten by other, more successful promotions for the same product. That hurts, but I learn as much from the losers as I do from the winners.

Whatever I learn, I make an effort to pass on to others through books, articles in the trade press, seminars, and speeches. I have written more than 30 books and 100 articles, most of them on marketing and other business topics. A few of these books are listed in Appendix 1.

In addition, I have seven years of experience running my own mail order business. It's called the Writer's Profit Catalog, and it is modestly successful. The Writer's Profit Catalog sells books, audiocassettes, and other information products for freelance writers and aspiring writers — mostly through small space and classified ads in writers' magazines such as Writer's Digest (see the example in chapter 7). Because I use mostly small ads (one inch and under), my advertising costs are minimal.

One of the best ways to learn mail order is by observing the activities of a real business. For that reason, I discuss the Writer's

Profit Catalog and its results in this book. You'll see reproductions of my ads, mailings, and catalogues. This will give you a good feel for how the mail order business works in the "real world."

A case-study, "here's what worked" approach is a lot more valuable than the theoretical approach you get in many classrooms. Believe me, I know. I once took a mail order course taught by someone who had never been in mail order. What a disaster! This is a subject theoreticians cannot tackle. It requires first-hand knowledge and experience, both of which I share with you in detail.

In addition to the Writer's Profit Catalog line, I have promoted a number of other products through the mail, with varying degrees of success. These include business books, audiocassette programs, special reports, and public seminars for consumers and businesses. I'll share information on these promotions and their outcomes with you, as well. I'll tell you why the successes worked and why the failures failed.

Another important thing to know about me is that I am not a big-time risk-taker. I don't have a huge bankroll. There's no family fortune or trust fund to back me up. We are not a two-income couple; my wife stays home with the kids. So we live on my income.

What kind of spender am I? I've gambled up to $5,000 on a single promotion, but no more. That's peanuts compared to what the big boys of mail order spend to test a new ad or mailing piece. One called me the other day to ask how to best spend $100,000 on an ad campaign for a mail order correspondence course.

But to me, $5,000 is a lot of money. Most of my ads cost under $200. Most of my mailings cost less than 60¢ apiece to send out.

I run my mail order business on a shoestring, with almost no financial risk, and that's the way I'll show you how to do it, too. Mine is not a get-rich-quick approach, because get-rich-quick can make you poor in a hurry if things don't go right . . . and they sometimes don't.

I will show you how to start small — and slowly. You'll advertise on the Internet for free. Your first magazine ads will cost under $100. Test these tiny, inexpensive ads until they begin generating a profit. Then expand into bigger ads, mailings, and other promotions using the profits you make from your early ads. I'll show you how to print your first small catalogue for under $300 and how to do very inexpensive mailings. This way, you won't put your life savings or house at risk. I know I sleep better this way. And I think you will, too.

If you're more of a gambler, you may choose to skip these early phases and start bigger.

Whatever approach you take, use only "risk capital" to launch your mail order business. Risk capital is money you can afford to lose entirely without adversely affecting your family or lifestyle. That way, a failed ad or a mailing that bombs won't disrupt your life or cause you personal misery.

When I started, I could afford to gamble only a few hundred dollars, and no more, on an ad that might or might not generate response. Some of my early ads did very well. Others bombed because of my lack of experience and knowledge. One $50 classified ad generated more than $800 in sales, while a similar ad in the same publication generated only $14. As I'll stress throughout this book, you never know what result you will get until you test.

Determine how much you can afford to risk testing your mail order ideas, and set aside the money for that purpose. If you make profit, great. If you lose it, life goes on.

c. YOU CAN SUCCEED IN MAIL ORDER

One of the reasons I am so passionate about helping people get started in mail order is that it is one of the few businesses the average person can get into without venture capital or other outside financial assistance, and make a five-, six-, or even seven-figure income working from home or a rented office.

Mail order entrepreneurs come from all walks of life. Many are salespeople who tire of being on the road, making cold calls, pressuring customers, and being rejected.

Many are families who work together at home doing the mail order business in their spare time, after school and their day jobs. It's a fun family activity to ship products and open envelopes with checks in them. (My seven-year-old son enjoys opening inquiries with me.)

Some mail order businesses are run by retirees who want to keep active in business but not be hassled with long hours, commuting, and dealing with clients and bosses. Mail order is the ideal spare-time business opportunity . . . you can be as busy and as active (or inactive) as you like.

Some mail order entrepreneurs are corporate dropouts. Many people who leave corporate life because of downsizing or reengineering become consultants or run other types of service businesses. But some decide to sell products via mail order from home. Ed Werz, for example, left his corporate job to start a successful mail order catalogue selling educational products to schools. When I saw him last year at a direct mail industry meeting, his business was prospering and he was brimming with enthusiasm.

Another type of mail order entrepreneur is the writer turned self-publisher. Books, pamphlets, reports, and other written information sell very well by mail. Writers can self-publish their writing, then market it through mail order ads and direct mailings. Sometimes they make more money this way than if they had been published with a big publishing house.

The key is interest and desire. If mail order fascinates you, and you dream of starting your own mail order business, you are a good candidate to do so.

d. STUDY DIRECT MAIL FLYERS AND ADS

Mail order does not require a lot of formal education. Much of the business can be learned through reading and observation. Do you pay attention to direct mail flyers, catalogues, and those full-page mail order ads in the Sunday supplement magazine? Studying these mail order promotions is like getting a graduate-level education in the subject for free.

Pay particular attention to mailers you get multiple times and ads that run again and again. These are examples of successful mail order promotions. How do we know this? Simple: if they were not successful, these companies would not repeat them.

4

Unlike general advertisers, mail order advertisers know fairly quickly whether an ad or mailing is profitable. That's because our ads generate inquiries and orders directly — unlike general advertising, which primarily builds brand awareness and company image.

If an ad doesn't generate enough orders to pay for the cost of insertion, we don't run it again in that publication. We try another publication, or rewrite the ad and test a new approach.

So remember: those mail order promotions you get again and again are the ones that worked. Study them carefully, and analyze what makes them appealing. Keep on reading direct mail and mail order ads. Watch more infomercials. And read the books and magazines listed in Appendixes 1 and 2.

e. HOW MUCH MONEY CAN YOU MAKE?

In the hype promoting mail order as a business opportunity, you will often hear that mail order has unlimited profit potential. This is one claim that is basically (and amazingly) true.

Can you get rich working for someone else? Yes, but people who do are the exception, not the rule. The chief executive officers and other senior executives of the Fortune 1000 corporations earn hundreds of thousands, even millions, of dollars in salary and bonuses each year. Other executives and managers earn handsome salaries of $75,000 to $200,000 a year. But the average worker in North America makes much less — somewhere between $20,000 and $40,000 a year. You'll make a decent living in that range, but you won't become rich unless you inherit a fortune or win the lottery.

The alternative? Go into business for yourself. You still may not end up rich, but the potential to make millions is there.

Many people starting a business go into personal or professional services: running errands, baby-sitting, typing, word processing, bookkeeping, wedding consulting, and so on. That's because service businesses are among the easiest and least expensive to start.

But the problem with service businesses is that you have a limited amount of time each day and a limited number of hours in the week you can sell to clients, so your income is severely restricted. For example, if you charge $10 per hour for typing, and you can put in 25 billable hours a week, you cannot make more than $250 a week unless you subcontract work to other typists or hire employees.

Mail order doesn't have this limitation. For example, I have small ads in one magazine that generate sales of about $2,000 a month. If you can do this in large markets, your income potential is almost limitless. For instance, if there were ten magazines covering the market segment for my product, it wouldn't take any more time or effort to run the ad in all ten rather than just one. And if the ad generated equal results running in all ten publications, I would be producing sales for this product of $20,000 a month for about the same effort it now takes me to make $2,000 a month. You can't easily do that in a people-oriented, labor-intensive business such as personal services.

How much money will you earn? It depends on how much work you put into it, how good your product is, how effective your ads and mailings are, and luck and timing.

Home Incorporated, a small business newsletter published in Baltimore, Maryland, reports that the annual earnings potential of a mail order business can be $500,000 or more. It estimates start-up costs at $1,000 to $10,000.

Jerry Buchanan, publisher of the *Information Marketing Report* newsletter, used to advertise his newsletter on marketing information by mail order (formerly called Towers Club USA) with ads saying you could make $500 a day. That's a pretty reasonable figure for the small-time or spare-time mail order operator. If you make $500 a day in sales five or six days a week, you gross $2,500 to $3,000 a week. For a 52-week year, that's annual gross sales of $130,000 to $156,000 a year.

What will your profit be? We'll discuss profit margin in detail later on. But a 40% to 60% profit margin is not unreasonable for a small mail order operation. At 60% profit margin, $156,000 gross sales generates profits of $93,600 a year. At 50%, $130,000 annual sales gives you annual profit of $65,000.

Those aren't bad numbers for a business you can run from your home in your spare time. They represent a handsome second income that adds tremendously to your regular paycheck or if, like many people, you can get along nicely on $65,000 to $93,600 a year, you could quit your job and just live off your mail order income if you wanted to.

I personally know a number of entrepreneurs who have made millions of dollars through their mail order businesses. On the other hand, many families and individuals are content to earn an extra $10,000 to $50,000 a year with a home-based, spare-time mail order business. It's up to you.

f. ADVANTAGES OF THE MAIL ORDER BUSINESS

Mail order is absolutely one of the best businesses I know of. Many people who are in professional-service businesses are under constant pressure from deadlines and client demands, and lead stress-filled lives. Store owners find retail tremendously competitive, and many have a hard time staying in business. Manufacturing has its own headaches, mostly associated with running a larger business with a staff of factory workers and meeting environmental and safety codes.

Alternatively, mail order can generate a handsome income in a relatively stress-free work environment. It's an unusual business. Instead of dealing with all the customer hassles of other businesses, you go to an office and dream up promotions. If your promotions work, you open envelopes and cash checks and money orders. An oversimplification? Of course. But not by much.

1. Mail order is not labor intensive

Mail order is not labor intensive. The bulk of the work — fulfilling inquiries and orders, picking and packing, shipping products, keeping records, maintaining product inventory, buying supplies, coordinating printing and mailing — can be done by relatively low-paid help such as high school or college students, homemakers who want to stuff envelopes in their spare time, people with physical disabilities, and retirees. You might also contract with word-processing services or small service bureaus to help out with some of the jobs.

As the owner, you are the "idea person." You decide what markets to go after, what products to sell, where to advertise, and

6

how to market and promote your goods. Unless you enjoy writing and desktop publishing, you can hire others to write your sales letters and design your catalogues and flyers for you.

The number of hours you spend on the business can be minimal. Legend has it that Paul Michael, one of the great mail order entrepreneurs, spent only an hour or two a day at the office, yet became fabulously wealthy. The Writer's Profit Catalog grosses in the mid five figures, yet I spend only a couple of hours a month on it. The rest of the work is handled by assistants and an outside mail-processing service.

2. Mail order is not service intensive

Mail order is not service intensive. As a freelance mail order copywriter, one of my great frustrations is having to turn down lucrative writing assignments because I am too busy. It's ironic. You work years to build a reputation and generate demand for your service. But when people want you, everyone seems to want you at the same time. In order to meet deadlines, you must limit the work you take on and turn away people who want to write you checks.

Mail order has no such frustrations. If I suddenly have a big surge in demand for a product, I can manufacture and ship as many as are needed. I can accept every customer's check. No one gets turned away. Promotional efforts that generate demand are not wasted; every inquiry can be fulfilled for a profit.

3. In mail order, you can take holidays

Another wonderful aspect of mail order is that there are not constant deadlines, demands, and pressures. As a freelance mail order copywriter and consultant, my week is filled with deadlines, meetings, telephone conferences, and writing tasks. As I write this, I am in my office on a beautiful June Saturday morning . . . because a client needed to consult with me in person and this was the only time available this week.

Mail order has no such pressures. I have an outside service handle all orders and inquiries. All I do, literally, is open envelopes and cash checks. I don't need to work long hours or be locked into a rigid schedule. Mail order entrepreneurs can come and go as they please.

As a copywriter and consultant rendering a service, I find it extremely difficult to take a holiday. Clients always want access to me, so I rarely take a week off — most of our vacation trips occur on long weekends and, even then, I am always in touch with the office via voice mail and my secretary.

Also, as a consultant, I make no money those days I am out of the office. The late Howard Shenson compared this dilemma to that of a dentist, calling it the "drill and bill" syndrome — unless dentists are drilling, they aren't billing. Even though dentists are well paid, they are in essence hourly laborers, which puts an upper limit to the income of a sole practitioner. So it is with any individual selling his or her services.

Mail order entrepreneurs can take a vacation whenever they want, for as long as they like. Orders continue to pour in and can be fulfilled by clerical staff while you are away. There are rarely emergencies that require your presence. In many ways, it's a wonderful life.

4. You can live where you want

And it's a life you can live where and as you please. Corporate employees and people selling services must usually live within driving distance of employers and customers. In mail order, your customers are all over the country . . . maybe even all over the world. They never see you, and you never see them. All transactions are done by mail.

Consequently, you can live wherever you want. Many mail order entrepreneurs choose rural locations, so they combine a handsome income with a lower cost of living than they would face in an urban center. My friend Joe Barnes, one of the old pros of the mail order business, lives and works on a large rural estate in the Adirondacks where, he says, "peace and tranquillity reign supreme." Another colleague runs a mail order business from a fabulous house with a breathtaking view of the Pacific Ocean.

With a mail order product, you can do business with anyone in North America, unlike a retailer, whose customers come almost exclusively from the local area. Mail order entrepreneur Bob Kalian describes the mail order business as "having a store with more than 260 million prospective clients walking by."

5. After set-up, mail order runs itself

Now let's talk about the hours required to start up and run the business. Let's compare service businesses with mail order again. A service business takes little time to set up and launch. Basically, you need a phone and a business card and you can start. After that, though, it's labor intensive. If you charge $50 an hour, you must work two hours to get $100.

A mail order business takes an enormous investment of time up front to get going. You must design, build, produce, write, or find and source products to sell.

You must create ads, brochures, catalogues, and sales letters. You must research the right mailing lists and publications in which to advertise. You must test various offers, copy, prices, and sales appeals until you find something that works. Dozens or even hundreds of hours can be invested before you make a significant profit.

Several times I have invested significant time creating a product that did not turn out to be a good seller. Many of the bigger players risk $25,000 to $100,000 on each new mail order idea. And not every product or promotion will be a hit. So you spend a lot of time creating.

However, once you hit on a successful combination of a good product and an ad or mailing that generates a lot of orders, the business can run on automatic pilot from that point on. True, you have to keep and check records to ensure that results continue to be profitable. And you should continue to test new ads and mailers. But often when you have a winning ad or mailing, you can run it for years without change.

My ads in *Writer's Digest*, for example, continue to pull well, even after running unchanged for seven years. No labor or thought on my part is involved in running them. Once a year, I send *Writer's Digest* a check to pay for 12 months of advertising, and that's it. A clerk responds to the inquiries and fills the order. I do nothing but collect the profits. Sounds good, you say? It is.

g. DISADVANTAGES OF THE MAIL ORDER BUSINESS

There are not many disadvantages to the mail order business. The main ones are described below.

8

1. Sales tax

You must collect and pay sales tax in certain states and provinces, depending on where your business is located (more about this later, in chapter 2). Doing so can be a paperwork headache. Also, the U.S. government periodically threatens to require mail order entrepreneurs to collect sales tax in every state, which would mean even more paperwork. Use of mail order software can save you time and simplify the situation. Taxes for Canadian mail order businesses, and details on paying U.S. sales tax, are covered in chapter 2.

2. Cash flow

In mail order, you usually pay the costs of doing a promotion before getting any money out of it. This creates a cash-flow problem for undercapitalized, small firms. The solution is to start small, then use the profits from your early promotions to finance later efforts. Growth this way is slower but safer. It's a problem only if you go into mail order full time at the beginning and need to make a living from it right away.

3. Legal aspects of working from home

Most small mail order businesses are run from the entrepreneur's home, and most of these homes are not zoned for business. In many cases, federal and local governments restrict certain business activities in residences. In chapter 2, I discuss the legality of operating such a business from your home.

4. Isolation of working from home

As a mail order entrepreneur, you will mostly be working alone. You will have less contact with other people than will the typical employed person. At first you may welcome this, but after a time, the isolation and loneliness may become a negative.

An introvert and loner by nature, I was glad of the opportunity to avoid people and work pretty much on my own. But as the years went by, I found it quite lonely and wanted more contact with people. Be aware that working alone at home may not be the utopia you dreamed it would be.

5. Living outside the mainstream

Mail order entrepreneurs, often eccentric by nature, live outside the mainstream of the business world. People may view you as a curiosity and not take you seriously. Or they may be jealous. Some people feel it is unfair that you get checks and money orders when you are not working a regular job. Be prepared for negative reactions.

In reality, you know making money in mail order is no more unfair than collecting interest on a certificate of deposit, selling property at a profit, or buying a stock that then increases in value. However, some people will feel you are cheating or avoiding useful work.

6. Increasing regulation and government bureaucracy

Federal and local governments are making it increasingly difficult for people to run mail order and other small businesses from home. Society as a whole favors the corporate employee and is structured against entrepreneurial types. For example, when I bought my home 12 years ago, I had difficulty getting a mortgage. Reason: the banks didn't want to loan money to a self-employed, mail order writer, even though I was earning four times my previous corporate salary.

7. Liability

You may be liable if a customer is harmed or otherwise damaged by a mail order product you sold him or her. Depending on how your business is structured (again, see chapter 2 for details), you may be personally liable, in addition to being liable as a business entity.

You must be careful what you sell people. For example, if you sell a booklet called *Alternative Treatments for Cancer*, and a reader dies because you told him or her to stop seeing a doctor and take wa-ba root juice instead, could you be sued? Think about it. And be sure to consult a lawyer knowledgeable in direct-marketing law.

h. WHAT YOU NEED TO KNOW BEFORE YOU START

Here are some answers to common questions for you, the start-up direct mail entrepreneur.

1. How long will it take to turn a profit?

When will you turn a profit? This is a tricky question. The answer is: as soon as you have a promotion that works.

Some mail order entrepreneurs have success with their first ad or mailing. Others lose money and don't make a profit until their second, third, or fourth effort, or later. My first ad bombed. My second ad generated in sales more than ten times its cost.

You can, as I did, start a mail order business on a shoestring — for under $200 — but if you have limited capital in the beginning, you will build sales and profits slowly. If you have more capital to invest up front, you can build sales and profits more quickly.

A small, inexpensive classified ad entails little risk, but even if it's very profitable, it generates modest gross sales per insertion. A full-page ad is more risky but can put thousands of dollars in your pocket in just a few weeks. Which approach is best for you? You decide. My personal preference? Get rich slowly, and don't take big risks with your savings and your style of living. But then again, I'm not a gambler by nature.

I advise you to start your mail order business in your spare time and keep your full-time job until the mail order is generating enough income to support you in the style to which you have become accustomed. You should also ensure you have enough savings to live without income for 6 to 12 months, in case you have some mail order promotions that bomb and cause your sales to decline.

Expect income to be modest at first. Many mail order businesses begin as spare-time ventures because, and while $10,000 or $30,000 per year gross sales is a nice second income, it's not enough for most of us to live on. Build from there and eventually you will be able to go full time into mail order if you want to.

If you decide to quit your job cold turkey and go into mail order full time right away (and I advise against this for most people), make sure you have enough savings to live without income for at least 12 months. It would help if you had an additional $10,000 to invest in mail order promotions, since you will need to generate income faster than a person doing this in his or her spare time.

2. How much money will it cost to start?

How much money will it take? It depends. With the increase in computer and office equipment on the market today, it's easy to spend $5,000 or even $10,000 setting up your home office before you make your first dollar in sales. If you have the money, that's fine. In fact, I advise those who can afford it to have a fairly well-equipped office, as outlined in later chapters, with the latest software and computers.

But the fact is, these items, while big productivity boosters, are not necessities. If you are on a shoestring budget, you can start your mail order business for $200 to $1,000. Here are some of the things you will need:

- A space and table surface to work from

- A cabinet or box to hold files

- A telephone

- A supply of envelopes, letterhead, and promotional circulars for various products you sell

- Stamps, paper clips, and other miscellaneous office supplies

- Enough money to run a few small test ads — $100 to $400 should be sufficient to start

You do not need money to buy an inventory of products. As we'll discuss in chapters 4 and 5, you can start by selling the products of other companies. These companies will hold the products for you, then ship to your customer when you send an order. This is known as drop-shipping and eliminates the need to tie up money in inventory.

You don't even need promotional literature, except for envelopes and letterhead. Most of the wholesalers that drop-ship mail order products supply camera-ready flyers and circulars you can reproduce at a local print shop or right on your copier in small quantities.

Can you risk $200 to $1,000? If you answered yes, you can venture into mail order.

3. Can I do this from my home?

Another money-saving aspect of mail order is that you don't need to rent a fancy office — or any office, for that matter. A folding table in your basement or spare bedroom will do just fine. My mail order business is in two finished rooms in the basement, but your rooms need not be finished.

Many mail order operators who start small at home continue working at home when they expand, finishing an attic or basement for that purpose, or perhaps adding a studio over the garage. Only a few decide to buy or rent outside office space, and this is usually by choice, not necessity.

4. Can I do it in my spare time?

Yes, you can do this in your spare time. Keep your regular job, and run your mail order business evenings and weekends. It won't take all your free time; just a few hours a week.

Yesterday, for example, I got $515.36 in orders. It took two minutes to open the envelopes, sign the checks, give them to my assistant to deposit, and send the orders to my fulfillment house for shipping. That was it for my day in mail order. By comparison, I have many friends who worked the entire day, for eight hours or more, and then commuted an hour or two, and did

11

not earn that much money. Which lifestyle sounds better to you?

Remember: mail order is labor-intensive in its start-up, but once things are running, you don't have to work very hard.

5. Can I do this if I am not a risk-taker?

You may wonder if you can start a mail order business if you are not a big gambler. I know you can. Take me as an example. I am about as conservative and financially timid as you can get. I invested only $100 in my first ads. I was 37 years old before I bought my first stock. Even conservative people like us can manage a $100 gamble to start a business, right?

To be fair, many of the most successful mail order entrepreneurs *are* risk-takers. It's their nature. They routinely buy full-page ads at $5,000 a shot or spend $25,000 on a test mailing. That's too rich for my blood.

You don't have to do what they do. Numerous mail order entrepreneurs prefer less risky promotions and have become rich on them. Many make good livings running small classified ads and sending out inexpensive publicity releases — two skills you'll learn in this book.

You can do this without quitting your job and risking it all. If things don't work out in mail order, you still have a job, and you can always try again in a month or so. Nobody will know what you did or the results, so risks are minimal.

6. Can I do this if I am not a genius and have not invented a product?

You do not have to be a genius or an inventor to be successful in mail order. However, if you are good at coming up with unique products or are aware of a customer need and can design products to meet that need, you will have a big advantage.

You need not be a writer or an inventor. But it doesn't hurt if you are. Inventors have an edge in coming up with unique products that can be sold by mail order. Writers can produce original audiocassette albums, videos, reports, and booklets to sell by mail.

I am a writer, but I am not great at coming up with product ideas. Most of my writing is done under contract for publishers and clients who want specific things written. They usually come up with the ideas — not me.

Still, I was able to start and run a successful spare-time mail order business that brings me a nice second income. If I can do it, so can you.

Keep in mind that mail order success does not always require a new or original product. Sometimes, you can take an existing product and promote it for a new application. For example, Eddie Goldman of Cubex, in New Jersey, saw a large plastic tub one day. Eddie is in the ice business. He realized the tub was large enough to hold a beer keg surrounded by ice. Eddie did a mailing to liquor stores, offering a free sample of his newly dubbed "party tub," and got an initial response of 40%.

If you are not product-minded, you can be successful by being customer-minded. Instead of thinking of inventions, think of what people like you want and need . . . then sell it to them. Frank Reich, a private pilot and wealthy entrepreneur, nearly had an accident once because he inadvertently thumbed the wrong switch in his cockpit. He realized other pilots were likely to make the same move, so he invented and marketed a protective cover to prevent the switch from being turned on accidentally. Although Frank is a brilliant inventor whose mind is filled with product ideas, this device came out of a need he had personally experienced.

Everyone has a unique life. Look at yourself. What business, financial, family, relationship, personal, or other problem have you had that you were able to solve? If you have had this problem, many others have too, you can be sure. Therefore, you can package your solution as a product, book, or report, and sell it to others at a nice profit.

Can't come up with ideas for products? Don't despair. There are many existing products that can be sold profitably if marketed correctly. One mail order entrepreneur I know successfully buys out-of-print books in large quantities from publishers — these are remainder books that didn't sell in the bookstores — and markets them at a profit through a catalogue and mail order ads.

So do you need to be able to invent or design products to go into mail order? Not at all. You need only develop a sense for what people want and need, what will sell. That comes from practice and experience. You'll get plenty of both reading and following the advice in this book.

2
GETTING STARTED

What must the beginner do to set up his or her new mail order business? The tasks include:

- Choosing a company name
- Setting up office space
- Installing computer and phone systems and other equipment
- Creating letterhead and stationery
- Filing the proper forms and papers with municipal and other authorities
- Planning for various aspects of business ownership, including tax and legal consequences
- Getting a business bank account
- Applying for merchant status to accept credit-card orders
- Arranging for insurance coverage
- Hiring employees or independent contractors

I know I risk boring you by covering these mundane topics. They are not the lifeblood of mail order; they are the niggling details. However, as information entrepreneur and seminar leader Paul Karasik observes, "Success in business comes from doing the little things exceedingly well."

a. TWO BASIC RESOURCES: TIME AND MONEY

As you'll discover, the two basic resources of any small business are time and money. Every business has a limited amount of both, but in different proportions.

When you are starting a business as a second source of income, both time and money are limited. If you quit your job to go into mail order, or start it as a second career after retirement, you will have more time but probably even less money.

Once you become successful and your business grows, the opposite situation occurs. You suddenly have more cash on hand and things are not so tight . . . but you are too busy, and there is not enough time to do all the things you want to do.

The point: If you have a lot of money but limited time, you can hire others to do a lot of the work for you. If you have a lot of time but limited capital, you can put sweat equity into your business and do most of the work yourself.

You *cannot* become successful with a small business if you are unwilling to invest either time or money. Many people fit this category; they are unwilling to risk even the few hundred or thousand dollars

14

necessary to test some mail order offers. And they do not want to give up TV or whatever else they enjoy in their leisure time to work after work, as most people who hold a full-time job and start a business on the side must do.

More dreams of small-business success fail to become a reality because people won't put in the effort and give up too soon, than for any other reason. If you want the rewards, you must be willing to put in the work.

b. CHOOSING A COMPANY NAME

The name under which you do business is important in mail order, perhaps more so than in other fields.

Why? Because, unlike a retailer, you have no store or showroom with which to impress customers. Unlike a manufacturer or service company, you don't employ salespeople who dress well and talk glowingly about your products.

The primary way you reach potential customers is through the printed page — ads, letters, brochures, catalogues, and inserts. Your promotional materials determine whether prospects buy, and your company name and logo are part of this package. While people care primarily about the product and whether it will meet their needs, they also care about the company they are doing business with.

People believe a product is more likely to be as advertised if it comes from a reputable company. They also believe a reputable company is more likely to honor its guarantees and provide good service.

But if your new mail order company is unknown, how are potential customers to know you are reliable? Nobody has ever heard of you and you have no reputation precisely because you are new. There are, fortunately, tricks of the trade you can use to make yourself seem larger and more well established than you really are. One such technique is to use an important-looking or attractive logo. Another is to give your company an impressive-sounding name. There are several options when it comes to business names.

1. Use your own name

Some mail order entrepreneurs do business using their own name. Melvin Powers, one of the most successful mail order entrepreneurs of all time, lists his company name as Melvin Powers on many of the books he sells by mail.

Using your own name gives an impression of a smaller firm, but one that provides personalized service and attention. It can be effective when you are selling products of a general nature, where a specific accreditation, credential, or expertise is not required. If your name is well known to a certain audience, using it as your business name takes advantage of this established credibility. If you use a made-up company name, your audience may not realize it's you offering the product.

You can always start by using your own name and change it later, or you can do business under your name, then start other companies or divisions using a variety of other names. Many mail order entrepreneurs use several different company names to promote different product lines.

Think about your audience and your product. For example, if you are a well-known motivational speaker named Ron Jones, it makes sense to have "Ron Jones"

15

in large type on the labels of the audiocassette albums of your speeches you sell via mail.

Other products and services require a more official-sounding name. For example, one of my clients, Norm, owns several banks. You wouldn't hesitate to open an account at his Sterns National Community Bank. If he had instead named it Norm's Bank, he probably would not have many customers. Obviously, the name you choose depends on the market and type of business.

2. Use a variation of your name

Joe Barnes, who writes and sells books via mail order from his mountain retreat in the Adirondacks, calls his company Barnes Books. Some other possible variations are Barnes Publishing or Barnes Associates. This combines the name recognition your name may have in a particular industry or market with the sound and impression of a larger company.

3. Use a made-up company name

Famous mail order marketer Melvin Powers eventually chose the name Wilshire Books for his mail order book business. Dan Poynter, who sells books and pamphlets on parachuting, named his company — appropriately — Para Publishing. Mike Weiner, a successful mail order entrepreneur, must not have liked the way his last name sounded, because instead of Weiner Publishing, he named his company Allen Publishing. He says it just sounded good to him.

These names sound impressive and are especially useful if your name, like mine, doesn't have a ring to it. The downside, of course, is that recognition of your own name doesn't carry over into the made-up company name.

4. Use an official-sounding institute or association name

When I went into the business of selling training seminars to corporations by mail, I saw that training directors wanted to deal with a company, not an individual. So I started doing business under the name (which I still use) The Center for Technical Communication. Who would you turn to for expertise in technical writing — Bob Bly or The Center for Technical Communication?

Andrew Linick, an extremely successful mail order entrepreneur who sells information on how to make money taking photographs, uses the company name The National Photographers Institute. When he started a business to help freelance copywriters find work, he named it The Copywriter's Council of America. Andrew is an expert at picking company names that connote expertise and credibility and that awaken trust and comfort in buyers.

If your name is Joe Jones and you are selling horoscopes by mail from your home in Montreal, you could call your company Jones Publishing. But is there a better, more official-sounding name you could use to make prospects feel you are a reliable source for this type of product? How about The Montreal Institute for Astrological Studies?

5. Use a logo

If you are using an official-sounding name to create a certain image, you can enhance that image by using a logo. Most big companies do. Most small companies don't. So if you use a logo, you appear bigger than you really are.

Any advertising agency or graphic design studio can design a logo for you. Cost varies widely. NBC reportedly paid a million dollars for their redesigned logo. A local graphic artist should be able to create a simple logo for your business for between $100 and $600.

6. Register your name

When you use a company name, you must register it with your local municipality. Contact the county clerk or an official in a similar position. Ask what is required to register a business. The clerk can usually send you all the necessary forms. You may have to buy a "DBA" (certificate of "doing business as"), which shows that you are doing business under the name you have selected. DBA forms are available from office supplier stores.

Submit three completed DBA forms for approval. Once it's approved, you keep one form, the local government keeps one on file, and you give one to your local bank when you open a business account.

c. SETTING UP OFFICE SPACE

More than 90% of the mail order entrepreneurs I know work at home. They do this for obvious reasons: when you work at home, you don't pay office rent, you have a commute of less than 60 seconds, and your work is always at hand, whenever you feel like doing it.

One aspect of mail order that is especially attractive to people with children is the ability to be home with them. But working at home with preschool children can be difficult, as they demand your attention, make loud noises when you're on the phone, and do not realize that you are working and cannot be bothered. You will need to decide what works best for you.

In an article on working at home, published in *The Sprint Business Resource*, Sprint Communications advises home-based entrepreneurs to set up a separate defined area of the home as an office. "Create an office that makes you comfortable," the article suggests. "Don't pick out the darkest, ugliest room in the house, filled with cast-off furniture. Remember, you'll be spending most of your time there." Common choices include spare bedrooms, finished attics or basements, and garages.

I believe a comfortable working environment increases productivity; space and solitude also help. Do not have a TV in your office. Do have a radio or stereo if background music helps you work, as it does in my case.

Plenty of desk space and file cabinet storage also boost productivity. There's room to organize and store work materials so they're close at hand and easy to find. Having to search for a book or folder wastes time and can cause you to lose your focus when you're in a writing groove. I have two desks and a large table in my office, so there is plenty of surface space for various mail order projects.

If you work at home, have two separate phone numbers, one for home and one for business. Make sure the business number is always covered by voice mail or an answering machine when you're away from your desk, and that it is always answered in a professional manner. At night, when you are done working, let the voice mail or answering machine pick up the business line unless you're willing to stop what you're doing and talk with the customer or prospect who is calling.

As your operation expands, you may find it taking over your house. Some mail order entrepreneurs eventually move their business to an outside office. I rented an outside office shortly after the birth of my first son. To my surprise, I discovered I liked working at an outside office. In my rented office, I write and think free of the distraction of my children, TV, and refrigerator. The quiet of an office away from the crowds — I'm on the third floor of a three-story building, so there's minimal traffic and noise — allows me to work uninterrupted. The separation between work and home helps me relax when I am done work and gives me a sense of privacy I wouldn't have if my business phone and fax were in my attic or basement instead of in a building two miles away.

d. ZONING LAWS THAT AFFECT HOME-BASED MAIL ORDER BUSINESSES

A common concern of home-based business owners is whether it is legal to operate a business from their homes. This concern became a plot device on TV's *The Drew Carey Show*. The main character runs a small brewery from his garage. When he dates a woman who turns out to be a zoning inspector, she issues him a citation which he has to fight in court.

The easiest solution to zoning problems is to rent an office in an area zoned for commercial businesses. If you live on a main street in the business district of town, your home may already be located in a commercial zone, making it a simple matter to get a permit to operate a business out of it.

Most of us, however, run our mail order businesses out of homes which are in residential neighborhoods. Zoning codes vary in different cities, provinces, and states. How do you find out what the standards are in your area?

To play it safe, don't notify your municipality that you already have a home-based mail order business. Make a discreet inquiry by calling the zoning board without identifying yourself, by having a friend or neighbor call the zoning board, or by asking a lawyer.

Some businesses are permitted to operate in residential neighborhoods. Generally, zoning codes will permit home-based businesses that —

- have few or no employees other than the owner,
- have few or no visitors,
- don't tie up traffic or street parking,
- do not pollute, generate a lot of waste, or produce a lot of noise, and
- are not outwardly visible.

Many home-based mail order entrepreneurs avoid the problem by keeping a low profile. As long as you don't disturb them, your neighbors are unlikely to complain. Other home-based mail order entrepreneurs check the zoning codes (which, in most towns, permit a mail order operation to be run from a home) and obtain the necessary permits and licenses from city hall.

According to mail order attorney Kalvin Kahn, in the unlikely event that your mail order business is not allowed under the zoning code, you can either ask the zoning board for a variance or you can modify your business operations to achieve compliance. For instance, if there is a problem with the inventory of products you store at your home, you can eliminate this by switching to an outside fulfillment service.

18

e. SET UP BUSINESS SYSTEMS THAT WORK

At the beginning of the chapter, I quoted Paul Karasik's comment that "Success in business comes from doing the little things exceedingly well." I learned, somewhat late in the game, the importance of getting these details right. The creativity of mail order is the fun part. The money in your mailbox may be what excites you. But keeping good records and having efficient business systems that work determine whether your business is profitable. The right systems can dramatically increase profits, improve customer service, save you time and headaches, and generally make your business run more smoothly.

Not having good systems for handling money, orders, and customer inquiries will result in unhappy customers, increased paperwork, and less-than-exemplary customer service. You'll have more problems, and running the business will be far less enjoyable for you.

You must create systems for doing routine tasks. A "system" is a standard procedure. Ideally, procedures should be written down. That way, you can give the instructions to employees and have them do the work for you. For example, my company offers several different products, each with a different brochure. Some inquiries are fulfilled with one brochure, others with multiple brochures, depending on which ad the prospect responded to (which you can determine by adding a key code to your address in the ad, as discussed later in the book, in chapter 14). We keep a notebook that shows, by source of inquiry, what literature my fulfillment bureau is supposed to send. It's all spelled out so even a new employee can fill the orders correctly.

I learned the importance of systems from bitter experience. Sloppy record-keeping wasted hundreds of hours of my time and cost me thousands of dollars in lost revenues and extra expenses. Only now, years later (better late than never, right?), am I paying attention to improving business systems. And each time I make an improvement, it pays off in money and time saved.

Organize your files so you have easy access to information on any specific order or customer, as well as summary information such as quarterly sales, annual sales, sales tax collected, inventory, and number of units of each item sold. You can keep these records manually or on your computer (see section f.1.) using any of the software programs listed in Appendix 3.

Information retrieval is a customer service function as well as an administrative function. If a customer writes to complain about an order, you must reply immediately to tell him or her when it was shipped, how it was sent, the items ordered, and other details. If you can't rapidly and easily retrieve this information, you'll delay answering customer inquiries — and this will create customer dissatisfaction.

f. EQUIPPING YOUR OFFICE

1. Computer requirements

Must you use a computer to operate a mail order business? No. Should you? Yes.

Everything you need to do in your mail order business can be done manually using pen and paper. I will give you all the necessary forms and instructions, so if you want to work without a computer, you may do so.

A computer, however, will be of great value in your business. Word processing, desktop publishing, mail merging (i.e., merging individual names and addresses with a form letter to personalize the letter), data base, communications, and other applications software can make virtually every facet of your mail order business run more smoothly and productively. For example, when customers call to check the status of an order, they want answers right away. It takes time to track orders using paper filing systems, but with a personal computer the data is at your fingertips in seconds.

Should you buy Macintosh or IBM-compatible? Many mail order companies have one of each. You can do nicely with either. Some mail order operators prefer the Macintosh because it is considered superior for graphics and desktop publishing. However, an IBM-compatible running Windows can run a variety of word-processing and graphics programs with powerful desktop design capabilities.

I have an IBM-compatible because of the consulting and copywriting work I do. Most of my corporate clients use IBM. Ad agencies and graphic design studios use Mac, but almost all can easily convert MS-DOS files to the Macintosh format.

Technology changes rapidly, so get a recommendation from your local computer store before you buy. Get the best system you can afford. If you buy an underpowered computer system, you'll probably need to upgrade it within a year. Upgrading means either buying a new computer (the most costly option) or adding improvements (such as a faster processor or more memory) to your existing machine. The company that sold you your computer can do the upgrading for you. If you are handy, get a how-to manual and do it yourself. If you're doing your own upgrading, I recommend the book *How to Maximize Your PC,* from Weka Publishing, a successful mail order publisher. Weka can be reached at 1-800-222-WEKA.

What system should you get? As of this writing, a high-powered home office IBM PC or compatible should come with at least 16 megabytes of RAM, 1 gigabyte or more of hard disk storage, a Pentium 100 megahertz processor, a four-quad CD-ROM drive, a 28.8 kilobyte-per-second (KBps) internal modem, a color monitor, and a 600 dots-per-inch or better laser printer. By the time this book is published, the new 56 KBps modems will probably be available at an affordable cost.

It is the software, not the computer, that enables you to perform specific tasks such as bookkeeping, mailing list maintenance, and desktop publishing. Following is a list of some of the tasks you can use your computer for, with suggested software. (Software can be purchased direct from the manufacturer via mail order or at a local computer or software store such as Comp-USA or EggHead.)

(a) **Writing.** Mail order is a word business. You will do a lot of writing — copy for promotions, as well as copy for products if you sell books, reports, and other information products. Any good word-processing program will do. I like Microsoft Word and WordPerfect, both of which have some built-in graphics capabilities. Microsoft Word, when purchased as part of Microsoft Office, allows you to incorporate Excel spreadsheets and PowerPoint graphics.

(b) **Research.** Learn how to do on-line research on the Internet by signing up with either a local access provider or one of the national services such as America Online or CompuServe. Spend some time exploring the various data bases, forums, and news groups.

At the same time, don't neglect basic library research. The library is a tremendous source of information, all of it free. Get to be on a first-name basis with the research or reference librarian. He or she can make your life a lot easier.

(c) **File transfer and e-mail.** You may want to send e-mail messages and files to customers, vendors, suppliers, and associates. For instance, if you are planning a new promotion and have just written the copy, you can e-mail it to your graphic artist in seconds, saving you a trip across town to the artist's office. An Internet connection with a local provider, America On-Line, or CompuServe will enable you to transmit e-mail messages and files quickly and easily, at minimal cost. Many service providers offer unlimited Internet access for less than $20 a month.

(d) **Desktop publishing/graphic design.** You can buy a desktop publishing program such as Ready-Set-Go, QuarkXPress, or PageMaker; learn how to use it; and do your own graphics and layouts. With a laser printer, you can even print out camera-ready pages that can be duplicated via offset printing or photocopying. Alternatively, there are many desktop publishing services that can do this work for you at reasonable cost.

(e) **Mailing list maintenance.** The mail order software listed in Appendix 3 can be used to manage and maintain your mailing lists. You should maintain a list of customers — those who have purchased from you — and "inquirers" — people who requested more information but did not make a purchase. You should be able to select names from the list based on whether they are customers or inquirers, the date of their last purchase, the items they purchased, and other criteria. For example, you might want to generate a list of all customers who bought from you two or more times. This is known in the industry as a "multi-buyer" list.

You need not buy specialized mail order software for list management. You can use a data base management program such as dBase or a contact manager such as ACT or Telemagic. Ask your local computer store for a recommendation.

(f) **Direct mail.** Most of your direct mail promotions will not be personalized. However, it's nice to have the capability to generate a personalized mailing to all or part of your customer list. The mail order, data base, or contact management programs referred to earlier can do this for you. The capability to write a sales letter and generate personalized copies to the people on your mailing list is called mail merge. Make sure the mail order software you buy has this capability.

(g) **Accounting, bookkeeping, inventory control.** The specialized mail order software listed in Appendix 3 typically has the accounting capabilities you need for a mail order business. Alternatively, you can buy one of the standard off-the-shelf accounting packages such as Quicken or Quick Books, or have a computer programmer customize a program for your business. One good source of customized accounting software is Plato Software (phone: 1-800-SW-PLATO).

(h) **Others.** Additional software will enable your computer to handle a wide range of other tasks. Ask your computer store for help.

2. Other equipment requirements

The tendency of beginners, especially those of us who are not wealthy, is to skimp on equipment and systems. There's nothing wrong with starting small and slow if that's the way you want to go. But practically every piece of hardware and software I've forced myself to buy has been worth its price many times over. For example, for years I kept my old thermal-paper fax machine because it worked well and I didn't want to spend the money on a plain-paper fax. But then I realized that my secretary was spending several hours every month photocopying the thermal faxes onto plain paper. I calculated I was spending more on her time and the wear and tear on my copier than the cost of a new fax machine. We bought a new plain-paper fax for $600, and it has already paid for itself in time and effort saved.

Leasing can let you get started fast without a lot of cash. If you don't have the thousands of dollars needed to buy the computer system you want, you can lease it for only a few hundred dollars a month. Fax machines, photocopiers, and other office equipment can also be leased. Most office equipment dealers offer leasing as an option. If yours doesn't, call a leasing company. One I recommend is Studebaker-Worthington Leasing Corp, (phone: 1-800-645-7242 or 516-938-5640).

(a) **Fax machine.** You need a fax machine. Any kind will do. Personally, I think it's worth spending a few hundred dollars more for a plain paper fax. Thermal fax paper curls and fades with time; the only way to prevent this is to photocopy the pages after you receive them.

Put your fax machine on a separate phone line. That's what businesses do, and you are a business.

(b) **Photocopier.** You can buy an inexpensive small photocopier for your office for under $1,200; a used machine should be fine. If you have information products, such as special reports, that you produce in small print runs, you may want to invest in a bigger, better copier and print them in-house, rather than take them to an outside copy shop or printer. Such a copier will cost around $2,000 or more. Remember that copiers can be leased as well as purchased.

(c) **Postage meter.** Another piece of equipment you will want to acquire is a postage meter. Each day you will take your outgoing mail and product shipments to the post office. Once your volume becomes significant, it will take too long to have the post office weigh the pieces and apply the postage. With a postage meter, you put on the proper postage yourself at your office, saving money and avoiding the wrath of other postal patrons and postal workers. The largest manufacturer of postage meters is Pitney Bowes (phone: 1-800-243-2300).

3. Do you need a toll-free number?

It is not necessary to have a toll-free number or even to take telephone orders. Many mail order businesses — especially those selling specialized information and other products through small, inquiry-generating ads — find that their customers prefer to mail in orders rather than call.

Toll-free numbers are available from your local telephone company or long-distance carrier. If you don't want the responsibility of answering a toll-free number, you can hire a fulfillment house to do it for you (see Appendix 8).

4. Purchasing letterhead and stationery

Once you've come up with your name and set up your office, you will need to order letterhead, business-size envelopes, mailing labels for larger envelopes and boxes in which products are shipped, and business cards. Your stationery's design can be simple or elaborate. It's up to you.

Shop around for envelopes and labels. Prices vary greatly, and as a mail order entrepreneur, you'll use a lot of these supplies. A good source for envelopes and mailing labels is Business Envelope Manufacturers. You can reach them at 1-800-275-4400 in Deer Park, New York. One mail order entrepreneur I know became a distributor for a box company so he could get a discount on the boxes he bought for shipping his mail order products. Smart thinking!

When you first start, order your pre-printed letterhead, envelopes, and business cards in batches of 500 or 1,000. In the beginning you may change design, phone number, e-mail address, even company name several times, and you don't want to be stuck with old letterhead you can't use. Once you are better established and your volume increases, you'll reorder envelopes and letterheads in batches of 1,000 to 2,000 or more.

Here's a useful tip: when ordering printed supplies, the more you order, the lower the cost per unit. If you are unsure of quantity, err on the side of ordering more rather than less. If you need around 500 copies of a flyer, for example, ask your printer to quote for 500, 750, and 1,000. Often the extra 250 or 500 flyers are only a few dollars more. It doesn't cost you a lot to have 100 left over, compared with the cost of going back to press for another run because you are 100 short.

g. TAX CONCERNS

As a small mail order operator in the United States, you must collect sales tax on orders placed by customers whose mailing addresses are in your state. Says mail order attorney Kalvin Kahn in his book *Mail Order Laws*, "You need not collect and pay the sales tax of the state of your purchaser unless you have a 'physical presence' — an office, warehouse, or salesperson — in that state."

This law has been challenged several times over recent years. It is currently still in place, but one of the greatest threats to small mail order operators is that the courts may some day strike it down. If a new law required you to collect sales tax in every state, the result would be an administrative and accounting nightmare. Order forms would have to be redesigned (and would be unbelievably complex) and computer software modified to account for the different sales tax rates in various states. Software and tax rate tables would have to be updated annually since sales tax rates do change periodically.

Canadian mail order operators collect the goods and services tax (GST) on all orders from customers within Canada. The GST is currently 7%. All provinces except Alberta also charge provincial sales tax.

Canadian mail order operators do not charge sales tax on orders placed by customers in the United States. U.S. mail order operators do not charge GST or any other sales tax on orders placed from customers in Canada.

In addition to sales tax, you must also pay income tax on your mail order revenues. The profit you make in your mail order business is considered income above and beyond the weekly paycheck you get from your day job and is, therefore, like your paycheck, subject to income tax.

When you receive a paycheck from an employer, money is deducted each week to cover the income tax payment. At tax time, you calculate your income tax payments. If you have paid more than you should have, you get a refund. If you haven't paid as much as you owe, you send the government a check to cover the balance.

Home-based entrepreneurs do not have income tax money taken out of the daily orders. Therefore, you must make "estimated payments" every three months, based on the total amount of income tax you think you will owe for the year. For instance, if you anticipate income tax payments of $8,000 for the year from your mail order income, you would pay the government $2,000 in estimated payments every quarter. Your accountant can set this up for you.

1. Does your business need its own bank account?

Should you open a separate bank account for your business? Yes. Business accounts usually offer less favorable terms (per check charges, lower interest rates, larger minimum balances) than personal accounts, but separating business and personal finances makes it easier to keep track of expenses and profits, measure your business's cash flow, and prepare information for your accountant at tax time.

2. Should you accept credit cards?

You don't have to accept credit card orders, but it's a good idea to do so. If you accept payment by credit card, it is easier for customers to place an order, and this will probably increase your response rates.

The major credit cards are MasterCard, Visa, American Express, and Discover. You will want to contact these companies and apply for merchant status, which means you can accept orders charged to their cards.

To get merchant status for MasterCard or Visa, contact your local bank. Be aware that MasterCard and Visa are often reluctant to grant merchant status to home-based mail order businesses. If your office is zoned for business, keep a small supply of your products available for walk-in sales at your office and apply as a retail business (retail businesses have a much easier time getting merchant status).

To apply for merchant status with American Express, call toll-free 1-800-528-5200. American Express seems to grant merchant status to home-based businesses more readily than Visa or MasterCard. However, you should try to get merchant status for all three. Discover and other cards are optional.

If you do not have merchant status with a credit card company but want to accept credit card orders, you can have a fulfillment house process the orders. These companies can, for a small fee, process payment for orders on their own merchant accounts and can even take inbound phone calls on their toll-free lines.

h. LEGAL CONCERNS

Every small business owner should have a lawyer. You will want to consult yours from time to time on a number of issues, including sales, copyright (as it applies to information products and promotional copy), income tax, and other regulations affecting home businesses.

One common legal concern is liability. Do you have any liability in your business? If a customer is harmed or suffers loss as a result of using your product, are you responsible? Can you be sued?

Actually, you can be sued by anyone, at any time ... and you must respond. This has never happened to me, and it's not likely to happen to you, either. But if it

happens, don't contact the person yourself. Handle it entirely through a lawyer. Chances are the lawsuit is frivolous and a firm letter from your attorney on his or her letterhead will end the matter.

For most mail order products, liability is not really an issue. For example, if you sell bulbs by mail and a bulb doesn't bloom, the customer suffers no harm or loss. At worst, you'll replace the bulb or refund the money.

Mail order entrepreneurs who sell products related to health or finances have more reason to consider whether there is any liability risk with their products. For instance, if you sell a home remedy or vitamin supplement and people taking your product say it made them ill, are you responsible? If customers lose money following the investment advice in your stock market booklet or from starting businesses according to plans you sold them, can they recover their losses from you? In most cases, no, but when in doubt, ask a lawyer.

Take a look at the disclaimer at the front of this book that tells you we can't guarantee your success and this book is not a substitute for professional advice and counsel. Add such a warning to any booklets, books, or other information products you sell.

Especially if you sell financial advice, there may be rules and regulations covering disclaimers that must be included in promotions. In the United States, for example, promotional claims for newsletters on commodities, stocks, and other investments are required to follow specific guidelines. Again, your lawyer can help you find out what these are and make sure you are in compliance.

i. INSURANCE

"Why would I need insurance for a home-based mail order business?" you ask. The chances that anyone would sue your business are indeed small. However, the fact that those small chances, if they occur, could result in big penalties is precisely why people have insurance in the first place.

What happens if the technician who comes to your home to fix your computer slips on ice on your sidewalk? You could be held liable and sued. A home liability policy usually covers this, but ask an insurance agent if your home-based business is covered by a residential policy or if you need separate home office insurance.

Home office insurance typically covers the replacement cost of damaged goods and equipment in case of fire, flood, or other catastrophe. Those of us who run our mail order businesses from our basements do risk damage to inventory and office equipment if the basement floods. Keep inventory on shelves off the floor.

If you live in the United States and your mail order business becomes so successful that you quit your regular job and become self-employed full time, you will need health insurance. The ideal situation is to be covered by the medical plan of the company where your spouse works.

Hint: Group insurance typically provides better coverage and costs less than individual health insurance. There may be groups you can join that offer good health plans at reduced group rates. Many entrepreneurs join such groups, not to participate in the group but primarily to obtain medical insurance.

In Canada, citizens are covered by their nationalized health plan, so obtaining or paying for basic health insurance or health care is not a concern (although residents of some of the provinces, such as British Columbia and Alberta, must pay insurance premiums to be covered by the plan). This is a major advantage Canadian mail order entrepreneurs have over their U.S. counterparts. Extended health benefits, however, can be purchased separately from private insurance companies.

j. YOUR PROFESSIONAL TEAM

When you are starting out in your own small business, you do not have the luxury of on-staff resources that you might have enjoyed as a corporate employee. As a result, you may find you do everything yourself, from sending out sales literature to packing products in boxes and taking them to the post office for shipping.

As your mail order business grows, you will get busier and busier. If you do mail order at night after your regular job, you'll be staying up later and later, and working Saturdays and even Sundays, to get everything done. If you are in mail order full time, you'll reach the point where there are not enough hours in your day to keep up with the orders. What do you do?

The solution is outsourcing. This means hiring others to do some of the tasks for you. But you don't have to hire full-time employees. You can hire freelancers or independent contractors.

Dick Benson, a well-known mail order consultant and entrepreneur in the United States, advises direct marketers to "buy outside" (outsource) all tasks and functions they can't do better themselves in-house.

3

HOW TO FIND OR CREATE PRODUCTS YOU CAN SELL BY MAIL

You want to make money in mail order, but what will you sell? And to whom will you sell it? There is a wealth of products and customers, but there are also some basic guidelines you should keep in mind as you choose products.

a. WHAT TYPES OF PRODUCTS CAN BE SOLD BY MAIL?

It is easy enough to find out what types of products sell best by mail. Start a notebook in which you list the different mail order products you see advertised in magazines and newspapers, promoted in direct mail, and featured in direct-response TV commercials and infomercials. You will soon have a large list of items that are being sold successfully via mail order. If others are selling these types of products, you can too.

Be careful of being an innovator. You might stumble on a product that seems ideal for mail order and speculate, "Nobody else is doing this, so I will capture the market." Maybe. But the big players may not be selling it for a reason. Most likely they are convinced it won't work. Or they tried it and failed. So be careful of being first. Be innovative in products but not product categories.

According to the late Eugene Schwartz, one of the most successful mail order entrepreneurs and copywriters of all time, the following products sell extremely well in mail order: books, clothing, jewelry, insurance, collectibles, newsletters, magazines, children's items, CDs and audiocassettes, automobile accessories, real estate, household accessories, electronics, status symbols, magic and superstition products, time-savers, and leisure-time products. To this list I would add hobby products, start-your-own-business plans, technical plans (for building your own house, helicopter, microbrewery), food, and gift items of all kinds.

b. HOW TO FIND A PRODUCT YOU LIKE AND ARE ENTHUSIASTIC ABOUT

Some mail order entrepreneurs do not care what they sell. What excites them is the mail order business itself — running ads, doing mailings, and then getting orders and checks in the mail.

Others get into mail order because they have an idea for a product they want to market, and mail order seems the easiest, best, most accessible way to sell it.

Many mail order operations grew out of one person's interest in a particular type of product. For instance, if you like engraved prints, maybe you can sell them to other art collectors via mail order. You have the advantage of going into the venture with knowledge of, and enthusiasm for, the product. The knowledge and enthusiasm usually come across in your communications with customers.

If you don't have a product you're in love with and want to sell, think of a problem you have that you want to solve. Is there a product that can solve it and that you can create or buy somewhere and sell via mail order? In chapter 1 I referred to Frank Reich, a mail order entrepreneur with a private pilot's license, who devised a protector for an airplane control switch so he would not hit that switch by mistake. He then used mail order to sell these protectors to other pilots.

c. CHARACTERISTICS OF THE SUCCESSFUL MAIL ORDER PRODUCT

Here's what to look for when evaluating products and their mail order potential. Your product does not need all of these characteristics to be successful, but it should feature at least some of them.

(a) **The product is not available in stores.** The easier the product is to get in stores, the more difficult it will be to sell via mail order. The ideal mail order product is available only by mail. The phrase "Not available in stores" is a magnetic lure to many mail order buyers. However, many products are sold both through retail and mail order. For these products,

the convenience of buying by mail order is what attracts buyers.

(b) **The product is story-rich.** This means there is a lot you can say about the product. The story can include how the product originated, how it was made, and, of course, how it benefits the user. Products sold through full-page ads and solo direct mail packages are usually story-rich, so the copywriter can weave a story that captivates and compels the reader to order. Catalogue products can be more like commodity items that are sold by showing a picture of the product, along with the price and a brief description.

(c) **The product can be priced for mail order selling.** A $6 product is priced too low to be sold profitably from a space ad or direct mail package. You can sell the $6 product profitably only if it's one of many items in a bounce-back or other catalogue (see chapter 4). Mail order products ideally sell for at least $10. If you are going to promote the product via direct mail, it should sell for at least $25 or more.

(d) **The product has an element of fun, mystery, or the unusual about it.** Mail order buyers like gimmicks, gadgets, and unusual or hard-to-find products. A good example is Ron Popeil's pocket fisherman, a fishing rod you can fold up and carry in your pocket. Rarities and collectibles sell via mail order. For example, one company sells lumps of coal allegedly from the sunken ship *Titanic*. Exclusivity and the promise of inside information also appeal to mail order buyers. An example is the *Boardroom Reports* promotion that begins, "WHAT THE AIRLINES DON'T TELL YOU…"

(e) **The product can be shipped.** Ice cream is not sold by mail because it cannot be shipped to the consumer without melting. Delicate, fragile, and oversize items are also difficult to ship. The ideal mail order product is compact enough to be shipped economically and rugged enough that it won't break or spoil in transit.

(f) **The product is refillable or requires updating or supplies.** I discuss in chapter 4 the importance of having additional products, known as back-end products, to sell your mail order customers. A refillable product, or one that requires updating, has its own back end built into it. A good example is a daily schedule. When you buy one of these calendars, the company gains a customer who will, in all likelihood, come back each year to buy refill pages for the new year. Another good refillable mail order product is vitamins. When you use up the vitamins, you have to order more to keep up with the regimen.

(g) **The product is different from competing products in at least one aspect.** Try to identify or create in your product at least one selling point that differentiates it from all other products in its class. Your copy will come across much more strongly if it focuses on an aspect of your product the consumer can't get when buying competing products. Hamilton Knife, for example, sells a machine-tool oil that makes tools last up to five times longer because of its superior lubrication. The lubrication is superior because the oil is literally magnetic, so it clings to the cutting edge better. In magnetic materials, the atoms are polarized, or aligned in one direction. Hamilton's ad headline — "Unique 'polarized oil' makes machine tools last 5 times longer" — capitalizes on the benefits of polarized oil compared to regular oil. This is Hamilton's unique selling proposition, which is explained at great length in the company's inquiry fulfillment materials.

d. WHO ARE YOUR CUSTOMERS?

It's impossible to stereotype mail order buyers, and you shouldn't try. However, many do have certain characteristics in common.

To begin with, mail order buyers are bargain hunters. Even though many products cost more by mail order than retail, the mail order buyer is looking for savings. That's why discounts and sales work very well with this audience.

Although people of all ages buy via mail order, many mail order buyers are in their thirties, forties, or older. Senior citizens are a big mail order audience. So don't set type in your promotions too small.

Mail order buyers are looking for items that are a bit interesting, different, or unusual. If there's a story to tell about your product, mail order buyers want to hear it. They like to be "romanced," talked to, and sold. Many are information seekers, and before they make a purchasing decision, they want more information about products than the average buyer does. Despite all the talk about illiteracy in North America, mail order buyers tend to be readers — more so than the general public. They will read your copy if it interests and intrigues them.

Mail order buyers are often people who either dislike retail or don't live close to stores. Mail order buyers look for convenience. They want to pick up the phone, call a toll-free number, give someone their order and credit card information, and be done with shopping. They like looking through interesting ads, mailings, and catalogues, but they don't get the same enjoyment in stores. Stores are too crowded, and they don't like dealing with store clerks; driving to, and parking at, the mall is a pain in the neck to mail order buyers. They're armchair shoppers. This is what you must keep in mind as you develop your line of mail order products.

4

PLANNING YOUR FRONT AND BACK ENDS

To succeed in mail order, you cannot have just one product. The majority of mail order businesses make the bulk of their profits on the back end — selling related products to people who have purchased the front end, or primary product.

The greatest expense in mail order is acquiring a new customer. Direct marketing expert Murray Raphel explains that it costs five times as much to acquire a new customer as it does to sell additional products (the back-end product line) to existing customers. Therefore, if you do not have a back end — additional products to sell people who have bought your main product from you — you are leaving a lot of profits on the table. And that's a mistake.

a. WHAT MAKES A GOOD FRONT-END PRODUCT?

A good front-end product has broad appeal to the majority of your target market. For instance, if you are selling advice on how to get a career in the travel and tourism industry, your front-end product could be a special report, "100 Best Careers in Travel and Tourism," since it covers all the career opportunities and therefore has the broadest appeal.

The front-end product should be of high quality and, if an information product, of substantial length and content. The price should be $15 at minimum and preferably higher — $20 to $30 or more. The selling price should be at least three or four times your cost of buying or manufacturing and shipping the product. Without this profit margin, you will lose too much money on your initial order to make the product a profitable front-end item.

You can quickly learn how companies put together their front- and back-end product lines by ordering some mail order products. Write down the name of each product and its price on separate pages in a notebook. Then keep track of other offers you get from the company. Record these products and their prices on the page under the primary product. This will give you a sense of how to structure front- and back-end product lines.

b. WHAT MAKES A GOOD BACK-END PRODUCT?

A good back-end product complements the front-end product. For instance, Dan Poynter of Para Publishing (1-800-PARA-PUB) sells as his front end *The Self Publishing Manual*, a book on how to self-publish your own book. Many forms are involved in publishing a book (e.g., copyright forms, ISBN registration), so a natural back-end product for Dan, which he sells from his catalogue, is a collection of all the necessary forms.

Jon Kremer of Ad-Lib Publications in Fairfield, Iowa, also sells information on how to self-publish and promote your own book. Recognizing that a major step in self-publishing is getting the book printed, he sells, as a back-end product, a directory of all the book printers in North America.

The Atkins Center in New York City publishes a newsletter, *Dr. Atkins' Health Revelations*. The Center's back-end products are vitamins and nutritional supplements recommended in the newsletter.

Back-end products should relate to the front-end product; that is, they address the same consumer need, fear, concern, or problem. If you sell vitamins, for example, a book on blood pressure is a good back-end product; a book on investing in mutual funds, unrelated to health, is not.

Back-end products are usually smaller than the main product, less expensive to produce, and priced lower (you should sell them for at least twice what it costs you to buy from the supplier or make yourself). This is not always the case. A percentage of customers who buy your product will buy a related product at a much higher price, and upselling your list on more expensive offers can often be profitable.

1. How big a back end do you need to be profitable?

The bigger the back end, the better and more profitable it will be. However, you don't need to have a complete back-end product line when you begin. Start with a small number of products, then add new ones as you create or find them.

For my Writer's Profit Catalog, where the front-end product (a cassette album and book) costs $49, my total back-end product line sells for more than $500, about

ten times the price of the front end. Individual items range from $7 to $59 in price.

If you sell a product in the $10 to $50 range as your front end, try to line up at least $100 to $200 worth of back-end products to start with. You can always expand later on.

Chapter 5 shows you how to create or acquire a wide range of back- and front-end products for your mail order line.

2. How do you offer back-end products to front-end buyers?

There are many ways to offer back-end products to front-end buyers. If you sell the traditional mail order method — through a coupon in an ad or a reply card in a direct mail package — sell only your front-end product in the initial promotion. Do not confuse the reader by adding back-end items on the coupon or reply form. The idea is to sell people the front-end item first, making them customers of your firm, and then sell them related products. If you try to sell more than one product in the first promotion, you will probably decrease your response.

3. The bounce-back catalogue

The greatest opportunity for selling back-end products is through your "bounce-back catalogue," which is a mini-catalogue of your entire back-end product line. It need not be elaborate; you can print it in black ink on white or colored paper (see my Writer's Profit Catalog in Sample #1).

A bounce-back catalogue should be included in every outgoing order you ship to your mail order customers. The beauty is that it promotes your entire product line at virtually no cost — there is no postage or envelope to pay for since it is mailed with

Writer's Profit Catalog™

Reports, books, and other information resources that help you get clients, gain confidence, and increase your writing income!

600-Series Reports

These special reports tell how to earn $100,000 or more as a freelance commercial writer—expanding on the material in Secrets of a Freelance Writer. *Each report is 8–10 pages.*

601 Tips for Beginners: How To Get Started in High-Profit Writing™

What if you have no experience, no portfolio, and no contacts? You can still get into high-profit writing quickly...but your strategy will differ somewhat from experienced writers. This report outlines methods beginners can use to hide, overcome, and even exploit their novice status including: How to generate lucrative business, regardless of your credentials...tips for writing sales letters that get clients to hire you...types of clients that hire beginners...how to create a winning portfolio of sample copy. $7

602 How To Set Your Fees...and Get Paid What You're Worth!

An in-depth discussion and explanation of how to determine, set, negotiate, and get your fees. Includes a survey of what top, intermediate, and novice freelancers are now charging for ads, press release copy, and many other typical assignments. If you're not earning at least $500 per day, you need this report! $7

603 How To Make $100,000 a Year As a Direct Mail Writer

Direct mail/direct response is one of the better-paying areas for freelance writers. This report tells what's going on in the direct mail industry today, how to break in, what the top writers are charging, how to get lucrative direct mail copy assignments. Find out why Bill Jayme gets paid $10,000 for writing a sales letter—and how you can, too. $7

604 How To Turn Dead Time Into Extra Profits

Every freelance writer will have periods when business is slow. This report tells how to use that "dead time" productively instead of sitting around and getting depressed. You'll also learn a simple technique that can prevent slow periods and virtually ensure a steady stream of work. $7

605 How To Double Your Freelance Writing Income—This Year!

Most writers don't have a business plan that projects cash flow. This report shows how to estimate your annual income based on your current fees, type of work you do, and how busy you are. Once I show you how much money you can expect to earn this year, I'll then tell you how to double that amount (no matter how much it may be). To do this, I charge only $7. Fair enough? $7

606 Bob Bly's Promo Package

This is the sales package I send to clients who request information on my freelance writing services. Estimating conservatively, I can confidently say it has generated at least $750,000 in direct sales of my freelance copywriting services and added 75 top companies to my ever-growing client list. If I were to write such a package for you as a client, my fee would be $3,000. Now it's yours for only $7. $7

607 How To Overcome Problems When Working With Clients

What do you do when a client doesn't like your copy, or won't pay your bill, or has an unreasonable deadline? What happens when an assignment turns out to be much more work than you bargained for—and you want to tell the client you are going to have to charge more than you originally quoted? How do you tell a current client that you have to raise your fees, or charge more than his budget for a particular project, or that you can't (or won't) handle his next assignment because you are too busy? In 11 years of freelancing I've been in just about every tough situation you can imagine...and in this report, I give you proven strategies for tackling each problem head-on with success. $7

608 Successful Moonlighting: How To Earn an Extra $2,000 a Month Freelancing Part-Time

Let's say you want to break into freelance commercial writing but can't (or won't) give up your current full-time job. Well, you can still make $2,000 a month or more in commercial freelance writing—as a moonlighter! What are the options for commercial writing on a part-time (evenings and weekends) basis? What are the limitations on the projects you can accept (e.g., you can't leave your office or talk with freelance clients during the day)? This report tells you how to avoid complications and earn a comfortable second income writing copy for local and national clients in your spare time. $7

609 Freelancing in a Recession

Is your business hurting right now? Are things too slow? This timely report provides 12 proven, practical strategies for surviving (and even prospering) in a recession, soft economy, or during a business downturn—12 action steps you can take to get more business *now!* $7

610 Government Markets for Writers

The U.S. government, with hundreds of agencies and 34,000 offices nationwide, spends approximately $14 billion a year on writing and editorial services. Most of this writing is done under contract by private organizations and often by individuals. This special report by Herman Holtz explains how to successfully find, bid for, and win government contracts for high-paying freelance writing assignments. $7

611 How To Make Money Writing Speeches

Freelance writers can make $1,000 to $3,000 or more for writing a 20-minute speech. In this report, veteran speechwriter Richard Armstrong reveals the secrets of how to succeed in the lucrative speechwriting market including: how much to charge...where the clients are...how to get assignments...how to research and write an effective speech...and much, much more. $7

612 How To Make Money Writing Annual Reports

Freelance writers are paid $8,000 to $10,000 and up for writing annual reports for major corporations. This report reveals how to break into this lucrative market including: who hires freelance annual report writers; how to reach them; what to charge; how to write annual reports; how to get an assignment even if you have never done any annual report writing before. $7

BBL-601.11

35

Writer's Profit Catalog™

700-Series

These reports are longer and more in-depth than the 200 and 600–series, averaging 30 to 50 pages or more. They are written by experts and tell you exactly what you must do to achieve the objective stated in the title of each report.

701 How You Can Make Big Money Writing Magazine Articles—NOW!

The traditional "one-shot," query letter approach to magazine writing won't make you rich. This report shows how to establish *long-term* relationships with editors who give you a steady stream of lucrative, ongoing assignments. Written by Steve Manning, author of 1,000 published articles, the report also includes Steve's proven 5-step article-writing formula, guaranteed to increase your output 10 to 50 percent or more. $19

702 How You Can Make $50,000 or More as a Freelance Copy Editor or Proofreader

Most proofreaders and copy editors barely earn a living. But some are making $1,000 a week or more. Learn how to set up and run a copy editing or proofreading business from your home that grosses $40,000 to $50,000 a year! Author Steve Manning's eye-opening report also includes complete instructions on how to properly edit and proofread manuscripts. $19

200-Series Reports

Want to write books, magazine articles, or other nonfiction material? These reports reveal the secrets of how to get your writing published. Most are from my popular Saturday seminar, "How to Become a Published Author"—which won't be repeated again for at least 2 years (so you can only get the information here). Reports are 5–12 pages.

201 Publish Your Way To Profits!

If you know something, one way to profit from that knowledge is to package it as a self-published book or special report—and sell it via mail order, distributors, and through other channels. My own self-published series of Special Reports brings in thousands of extra dollars in income a year—with virtually no effort. If you've ever had the urge to self-publish…or are just thinking about it…you need the information contained in this report. Written by Brooks Owen. $7

202 How To Get a Good Literary Agent To Represent You.

Once you have a good book idea and a proposal for it, you need to find an agent who can sell your book to a publisher and get the best deal for you. Fewer and fewer publishing houses nowadays will even consider a proposal unless it is submitted by a recognized literary agent. But where do you find agents? What's the best way to contact them? How can you get them to take you seriously? What should you look for in an agent—and what kind of results can you expect once an agent takes you on as a client? This report will answer these questions and help you get the agent you need. $7

203 How To Write Winning Query Letters.

Students at my writing seminars are amazed when I tell them that (with a few exceptions) sending a finished article to an editor who didn't ask to see it can actually prevent you from making the sale. Editors want to see a query first—and your ability to write persuasive queries will, in large part, determine whether you become a published and prolific magazine writer. This report shows you: How to write successful query letters…how to produce queries that make the editor think you've done a lot of research (even if you haven't!)…plus numerous sample query letters you can follow and adapt to suit your needs. $7

204 How To Make Money In the Public Seminar Business.

Giving seminars (on writing, publishing, communication, or any topic you choose) is an excellent way for you, the writer, to cash in on your ability to inform, entertain, educate, and communicate. Profits, in many cases, can exceed $1,000 per day, and you can even present seminars in your spare time (Saturdays and evenings) if you hold a regular 9-to-5 job. This report serves as the perfect introduction for writers who think they might want to make money in the public seminar business. You'll learn the steps to take—and the mistakes to avoid. $7

205 How To Write a Winning Book Proposal

If you want to sell your book to a publishing house and become a published author, you must learn to write effective book proposals. This is easy if (a) you know the steps involved in writing such a proposal, and (b) you have a sample book proposal you can "copy" and use as a model in developing your own proposal. My information-packed report fills both those needs. It teaches you step-by-step how to write a winning book proposal, and each section is followed by an excerpt from an actual book proposal. Once you have this report in hand you'll be able to easily and quickly translate any idea into a solid proposal ready to submit to agents and publishers. $7

206 $50,000 A Year Through Self-Syndication

This report provides step-by-step instructions on how to make money as a nationally syndicated columnist. It tells how to sell through major feature syndicates (King, United Features) as well as how to market your columns to newspapers and magazines directly. Written by Herman Holtz. $7

Full Length Books (300-Series)

300 Get Paid to Write Your Book

The definitive work on how to write a nonfiction book and sell it—for a nice advance—to a major New York publishing company. Topics include: coming up with book ideas, evaluating the market potential of your book, how to write a successful book proposal, how to get a literary agent to represent you, selling your book to publishers, and negotiating your advance and royalties. (NOTE: This book includes the complete text of Special Reports 202 and 205.)
Oversize paperback, 100 pages $22

301 The Copywriter's Handbook

While *Secrets of a Freelance Writer* tells you how to run your copywriting business, *The Copywriter's Handbook* tells you how to write effective copy for ads, brochures, catalogs, direct mail, press releases, TV and radio commercials, newsletters, speeches, and other projects your clients need. "I don't know a single copywriter whose work would not be improved by reading this book," says David Ogilvy, founder of Ogilvy & Mather. "And that includes me."
Trade paperback, 353 pages $15

302 Secrets of a Freelance Writer: How To Make $85,000 a Year

Do you want to make a *lot* of money through freelance writing? There are dozens of high-paying commercial writing projects and clients in your own backyard—yours for the asking. Step by step, this book reveals how you can make $85,000 to $125,000 a year or more writing ads, brochures, and promotional materials for local and national clients.
Trade paperback, 274 pages $13

Writer's Profit Catalog™

302-A Secrets of a Freelance Writer:
Book II: The Graduate Course
This money-making manual picks up where *Secrets of a Freelance Writer* left off, presenting dozens of strategies for earning $100,000 to $150,000 a year or more as a freelance commercial writer. Topics include: What to do when the client says, "Your fee is too high"...how to get clients to pay you to attend meetings with them...what to say when following up on prospect inquiries...contracts for freelance writers...how to say "no" without blowing the client away...and much, much more.
Oversize manual, 50 pages $19

303 Advertising Freelancers:
The New Lure of Freelancing
Everything about this promising work style as told by successful copywriters and art directors—and their clients, companies, and ad agencies. Read how dozens of independent-spirited creative people left the security of salaried jobs to control their own careers. Read, too, about the companies and ad agencies who hire freelancers: why they prefer to work with them, what they look for, how they approve the work, what they pay for it. Written by Ed Buxton and Sue Fulton.
Trade paperback, 114 pages $22

305 The Elements of Technical Writing
Freelance and contract technical writers can earn $25 to $80 an hour writing manuals, proposals, specifications, and other technical documents. And here's the style guide you need to handle such assignments with confidence. Covers use of numbers, units of measure, equations, technical terms, symbols, and other special concerns of technical writing.
Hardcover, 140 pages $20

306 Creative Careers: Real Jobs In Glamour Fields
A job-hunter's guide to ten of today's most exciting industries including travel, theater, photography, motion pictures, publishing, music, finance, gourmet foods, television, and advertising.
Trade paperback, 334 pages $12

307 Create the Perfect Sales Piece:
A Do-It-Yourself Guide To Producing Brochures,
Catalogs, Fliers, and Pamphlets
You can make $50,000 or more per year writing sales materials for clients. This book provides the step-by-step instructions you need to successfully research, outline, and write sales brochures, booklets, fliers, pamphlets, annual reports, catalogs, and many other lucrative assignments.
Trade paperback, 242 pages $20

311 How To Make Money Writing Technical Manuals
John Lancaster's clear, informed, well-thought-out book spells out everything you need to know about making money writing technical manuals. You learn who the clients are...how to find business...how to determine what to charge the client...contracts, advances, and payment schedules...submitting your bills and getting them paid...and much, much more.
Oversize paperback, 41 pages $31

312 Turbocharge Your Writing:
The Vitale Instant Writing Method
A 7-step formula for effective writing. I find it especially helpful when I'm faced with a difficult or intimidating writing assignment or am just having trouble getting started. This book by Joe Vitale is like a gem—small but valuable.
Paperback, 23 pages $5

313 How To Promote Your Own Business
A practical, do-it-yourself guide to advertising, publicity, and promotion for the small-business manager or owner. Lots of good marketing advice for promoting your own freelance writing business or the products and services sold by your clients.
Trade paperback, 241 pages $13

315 Selling Your Services: Proven Strategies for
Getting Clients to Hire You
If you sell professional, personal, consulting, trade, technical, freelance, or any other kind of service, this book will give you the information you need to get large numbers of prospects to call you, convince those prospects to hire you at the fees you want, and dramatically increase the sales of your services.
Hardcover, 349 pages $27

316 The Elements of Business Writing
The Elements of Business Writing presents the basic rules of business writing in a concise, easy-to-use handbook organized along the lines of Strunk and White's classic book, *The Elements of Style.*
Hardcover, 144 pages $20

317 Business-to-Business Direct Marketing
This book shows you how to improve results from business-to-business marketing communications including ads, direct mail, PR, brochures, catalogs, postcard decks, and more. Also identifies and explains the 7 critical differences between business-to-business and consumer marketing.
Hardcover, 267 pages $42

318 Targeted Public Relations
A no-nonsense guide to achieving maximum visibility, press coverage, leads, and sales from public relations done on a limited budget.
Hardcover, approx. 220 pages $25

319 Keeping Clients Satisfied
In today's economy, clients and customers want it better, they want it cheaper, and they want it *yesterday!* This book shows you the customer service techniques necessary to satisfying and retaining clients in this new competitive marketplace.
Hardcover, approx. 250 pages $27

320 Technical Writer's Freelancing Guide
A complete and authoritative guide to the lucrative form of freelancing known as *contract work,* in which freelancers are hired by companies to do technical writing—at a high hourly rate and for an extended period of time—working at the company's facilities (similar to being a high-paid "temp"). Written by Peter Kent.
Trade paperback, 160 oversize pages $15

321 Make Money Writing Newsletters
A complete guide on how to make big money writing promotional newsletters for local and national businesses. Author Elaine Floyd's ideas and tips are based on 5 years of operating her own newsletter production company with annual sales of $250,000.
Oversized paperback, 138 pages $32

322 Ghostwriting: How To Get Into the Business
Want to make big money ghostwriting books for celebrities, corporations, and individuals? This book tells how. Written by Eva Shaw.
Trade paperback, 185 pages $10

325 The Ultimate Unauthorized Star Trek Quiz Book
More than 750 trivia questions to test your "Trekpertise." Covers the Star Trek movies, TV shows, and novels.
Trade paperback, 162 pages $11

326 Power-Packed Direct Mail
Complete, easy-to-follow instructions on how to increase direct mail response rates. Covers planning, offers, mailing lists, testing, copy, design, formats, personalizations, and more.
Hardcover, 349 pages $27

Live Seminars With Bob Bly
"How to Make $85,000 a Year As a Freelance Writer" and "How to Become a Published Author."
For more information, call The Learning Annex at (212) 570-6500.

Writer's Profit Catalog™

327 Careers for Writers
The ultimate career guide for writers and those who want to become writers. Covers staff and freelance opportunities in book and magazine publishing, TV and radio, newspapers, advertising, film, corporate communications, public relations, technical writing, and more.
Hardcover, 198 pages $15

Audio Cassette Programs (800-Series)

**801 Secrets of a Freelance Writer: How to Make
       $85,000 a Year**
This audio cassette program is packed with my latest information and newest ideas on how to make $85,000 to $100,000 a year or more as a freelance writer in today's competitive marketplace. The program was professionally recorded "live" at my full-day Learning Annex seminars, now given in New York City just one or two times a year.
Six 1-hour cassettes $49

802 10 Magic Steps to Freelance Writing Success
Presents the 10 essential steps every writer must take to make the leap to an annual income of $100,000 or more and consistently maintain (or increase) that income, year after year.
Single cassette $12

803 How to Boost Your Direct Mail Response Rates
Proven techniques for dramatically increasing your direct mail response rates. Includes rules for testing, target marketing strategies, offers, list selection, design, copy, mistakes to avoid...and much, much more.
Single cassette $12

**804 Sixteen Secrets of Successful
       Small Business Promotion**
How to use low-cost/no-cost advertising, marketing, sales promotion, and public relations techniques to build your business. Learn how to: Gain credibility through public speaking. Generate thousands of leads using simple press releases. Get big results from tiny ads. And more.
Single cassette $12

805 Selling Your Services in a Soft Economy
How to successfully sell and market your freelance writing services in a recession or soft economy.
Single cassette $12

812   The Motivating Sequence
A proven, easy-to-follow 5-step formula for writing more persuasive sales letters, billing series, ads, mailers, and more.
Single cassette $12

814 Get Paid to Write Your Book
How to write a nonfiction book and sell it for a $5,000 to $15,000 advance to a major NY publisher. Covers book proposals, literary agents, royalties, book contracts, and much more.
Six cassettes $59

816 Selling Your Services
The complete text of *Selling Your Services: Proven Strategies for Getting Clients to Hire You or Your Firm* (book #315 in this catalog) on tape. Read by Jeff Riggenbach.
8 cassettes $53

Videos (900-Series)

901 How to Get Your Nonfiction book Published
This video, filmed live at Barnes & Noble, outlines the 5 main criteria by which publishers decide whether to accept or reject ideas for nonfiction books...and tells you how to satisfy each of the 5 requirements in your proposal to them. Also included: 10 proven techniques for generating saleable book ideas.
60-minute video, VHS format $24

Clip this coupon and mail it with your payment. (You may photocopy it, if you wish.)

Items you wish to order (indicate item #'s):   _____ _____ _____ _____

_____ _____ _____ _____ _____ _____

_____ _____ _____ _____ _____ _____

_____ _____ _____ _____ _____ _____

_____ _____ _____ _____ _____ _____

Name _____ Phone #_____

Address _____

City_____ State_____ Zip_____

Enclose money order, cash, or check (payable to "Bob Bly") for appropriate amount. NJ residents add 6% sales tax. Canadian residents add $2 (U.S. dollars) per order. 30-day money-back guarantee on all books and cassettes. All items guaranteed to please. **Please allow 2–4 weeks for delivery.**

❏ Please rush my materials. I've enclosed an extra $1 per book (300-series) and 50¢ per tape or report (200, 600, 700, and 800-series) for first-class delivery.

MAIL TO: Bob Bly, 22 E. Quackenbush Avenue, Dumont, NJ 07628   BBL-601.11

the product shipment. The only cost is the few pennies per catalogue for printing.

If a small, home-based mail order business includes a bounce-back catalogue in all product shipments, it can double its annual gross sales, or better, with virtually no added marketing cost.

You can promote your back end in other ways, of course. For instance, you can periodically mail your bounce-back catalogue or other special offers to your list of mail order customers. But the cheapest, easiest way to sell back-end products is to enclose bounce-back catalogues with products being shipped. If you don't do this, you are missing out on a large share of the profits your mail order business can generate for you.

4. How can you test back-end products inexpensively?

You can experiment with different back-end products in your mini-catalogue easily and inexpensively. When you find an item you want to offer, order a small quantity on consignment from the manufacturer or arrange for the manufacturer to drop ship to your customers (drop shipping is explained in chapter 5). This allows you to test a product without making any significant investment in inventory or product development.

Print a small quantity of bounce-back catalogues (I usually print 500) offering the products you are testing. If orders are good and the product is profitable, order larger quantities from the manufacturer at a deep discount, or you can continue to drop ship. Alternatively, develop and produce your own product similar to the one you tested.

If a product is not profitable, meaning people don't order it, return your consignment inventory and delete the item from the next edition of your catalogue.

Sometimes a back-end item sells well for a time, then slows down or is replaced by a newer, more appropriate item. You can always get rid of the remaining inventory by offering the item on sale at 10% to 20% discount or more.

Another strategy is to offer the old item as a premium, or gift. You tell customers that if they order a certain minimum dollar amount of merchandise from your catalogue, they will receive the item for free. This is effective in getting customers to place a larger order than they might have otherwise.

c. ADDING TO YOUR BACK END IS FUN AND PROFITABLE

Since the back end can be modified and expanded gradually, creating and building a back-end product line is one of the few things in mail order you can do at a reasonably leisurely pace. Once you have an ongoing, successful product line, it's fun to discover new products you can sell profitably as part of your back end.

If you sell information products and you come across an old book that looks like it would make a good back-end item, contact the publisher. If the book is about to go out of print or has recently gone out of print, you can often acquire both the remaining inventory and the rights to reprint the book at bargain basement prices. If the book has been out of print for a while, the rights may have reverted to the author. Contact the author and offer to buy any remaining inventory. If the book really sells, you can negotiate with the author to become the new publisher.

Keep in mind that back-end products usually fill a gap in the customer's requirements that the front-end product does not address. Often this need or requirement is, in fact, created by the front-end product.

For instance, if you sell sales training materials on how to sell more product by telephone, and your front-end product recommends use of a telephone headset, many of your customers will write you asking where they can get such a headset and which one you recommend. If you contact the manufacturer of your preferred brand of headset, you could arrange to become a distributor and sell the headset directly to your customers — and make the profit yourself — when they call looking for it.

d. TIPS FOR SELLING INFORMATION PRODUCTS

Many mail order beginners, as we have discussed, find selling "information products" the easiest and most inexpensive way to get started. Because information is an ideal product to sell via mail order, it's no wonder so many successful mail order marketers choose to concentrate on information products.

Is the information explosion a good thing for information marketers? Actually, it's a mixed blessing.

- People have too much to read and not enough time to read it.

- More and more information is competing for their attention.

- There is a proliferation of low-cost/no-cost information sources eating into the market for your expensive information products.

Fortunately, you can still succeed selling information by mail. It's tougher than it was in yesteryear, I think, but here are some rules and guidelines formulated specifically for information marketers competing in the Information Age.

(a) **Narrow the focus.** Although the most profitable product may be one with wide appeal, such as Joe Karbo's *Lazy Man's Way to Riches* or Bob Kalian's *A Few Thousand of the Best Free Things in America*, "goldmine" concepts such as these are difficult to come by. Today we live in an age of specialization. People have narrow, specific areas of interest and eagerly seek the best information in these niche areas. Match your own interests and expertise with the information needs of an identifiable market and you're on your way.

How big must this market be? Jerry Buchanan, publisher of *Information Marketing Report*, a how-to newsletter for information marketers and self-publishers, says that "any group large enough that some magazine publisher has seen fit to publish a magazine about them or for them" is large enough for your purposes.

(b) **Seize a subject.** The typical magazine writer or book author tends to wander from subject to subject to satisfy a never-ending curiosity about all things. The information marketer must behave differently. He must latch onto a narrow niche or topic, make it his own, and produce a series of information products that meet the needs of information-seekers buying materials on this subject. Not only does this increase profits by giving you more products to offer your customers but it also helps establish you as a recognized expert and authority in your field.

(c) **Plan the back end before you start marketing.** Many entrepreneurial direct-response advertisers dream of duplicating the one-shot success of Joe Karbo and of getting rich from a single mail order book, but it rarely happens. This front-end sale can be profitable if cost-effective marketing techniques are used. But the real profits are in the back end — selling a related line of additional information products to repeat customers. I advise clients to plan this back end of related products before launching a direct-response campaign. Precious opportunities for repeat sales will be lost if they can only offer a single product to information-hungry buyers.

(d) **Test your concept with classified ads.** Most information marketers want to mail thousands of direct mail packages or place full-page ads immediately. That's fine if you can afford to risk $5,000 to $25,000 on an untested idea. However, I prefer to test with small classified ads first (see chapter 7). By doing so, I can determine the product's sales appeal and potential for under $200.

Your ad should seek inquiries, not orders. All requests for information should be immediately fulfilled with a powerful direct mail sales letter, circular, order form and reply envelope (see chapter 8).

What should all this cost? A successful classified ad will bring in inquiries at a cost of 25¢ to $1 per lead. A good sales package will convert 10% to 35% of these leads to sales. I have run classified ads that pulled up to 17 times their cost in product sales.

(e) **Don't underestimate the importance of the bounce-back catalogue.** As discussed, a bounce-back catalogue is a circular containing descriptions and order information for your complete line of related information products. When a customer orders your lead product, you insert the bounce-back in the package and ship it with the order. Ideally, the customer sees the catalogue, scans it, orders more items . . . and the order "bounces back" to you.

Additional sales generated by bounce-backs can range in dollar amount from 10% to 100% of the front-end sales generated by your original ad or mailing. The only cost is a few cents to print each catalogue sheet. (**Tip:** When you fulfill a bounce-back order, send out another bounce-back catalogue . . . and another . . . until the customer has bought every item in the catalogue.)

(f) **Create low-, medium-, and high-priced products.** Different buyers have different perceptions of what information is worth and what they will pay. You will get more sales by testing a variety of prices for your lead item and by offering a number of different back-end products reflecting a broad range of prices.

My front-end product is a $49 cassette and book package. The back end consists of a series of $7 and $8 reports, a second book for $20, and a second six-tape cassette album for $49.95. Jeffrey Lant, who sells business development products and services, has products ranging from a $4 report to a $4,800 consulting service.

Recently, I sent an inquiry to a well-known and successful marketer who specializes in selling information on how to make money as a speaker. I didn't buy because the only alternatives were a large cassette album or a one-year newsletter subscription, both of which were fairly expensive. I wasn't ready to make that kind of commitment to the subject. Most buyers prefer to sample your information with a lower-priced product, such as a book, single cassette, or inexpensive manual in the $10 to $49 range.

(g) **Let your buyers tell you what products they want you to create.** Always put your name, address, and phone number on every information product you produce, and encourage feedback from readers. Many readers become advocates and fans, calling and writing to establish a dialogue with you. You should welcome this. Not only can you solve their problems and answer their inquiries by telling them which current products to buy, but their questions can suggest new products. Most of my back-end reports were written to answer specific questions readers asked me repeatedly. Instead of having the same telephone conversation over and over again, I can sell a report that contains the answers my readers seek. It saves time and generates revenue.

(h) **Be the quality source.** Your strongest advertisement is a good product. A clever or deceptive ad can certainly generate brisk sales, and returns may not be excessive even if your product is poor, but customers will feel cheated and will not favor you with repeat business.

A good product will have people actively seeking you out and will bring in a small but steady stream of phone calls, letters, inquiries, and orders generated by the product itself and not by the advertising. You would be surprised by the enormous effort some people expend to locate quality information products that are well spoken of by other buyers.

5

PRODUCING OR SOURCING YOUR PRODUCTS

You have picked a product, or you have an idea of the type of product you want to market. But where do you get it? You can either create and manufacture your own products, manufacture existing items, or purchase products from other manufacturers.

a. CREATE YOUR OWN PRODUCTS

If you create and manufacture your own products, you will have lower product costs than you would purchasing the product from a company that must charge a price to cover its costs and profit. Lower manufacturing costs give you a greater profit margin. You can sell the product at a high price and realize the profit yourself; you can also afford to charge less, which may be necessary as you try to find the optimum selling price.

When you make your own product, you control the supply. If your mail order business depends on a product sourced from a single manufacturer, you have a problem if that company stops making the product.

The easiest products to create are information products — booklets, reports, books, and other "paper and ink" products. You can write them yourself, print out originals on your laser printer, and reproduce them at a local offset printer, copy shop, or on your own copier.

Electronic information products such as CD-ROMs, software, videos, and audiocassettes are relatively easy to create and reproduce. These also make good mail order items with a low per-unit manufacturing cost and a handsome selling price.

Tangible goods such as food products, clothing, and collectibles are more complex to produce and ship, but you can do it. These items usually require a substantial up-front investment. Many mail order companies that sell tangible goods were already making these goods and selling them by other means before expanding sales to offer the product through mail order. A good example is Junior's Cheesecake in New York. Junior's makes what is arguably the world's best cheesecake (I've had it and it's delicious) and sells thousands in its Brooklyn restaurant each year. Many customers began asking how they could order additional cheesecakes to eat at home, and Junior's Cheesecake is now a thriving mail order operation.

b. BUY PATENTS OR COPYRIGHTS TO EXISTING PRODUCTS AND MANUFACTURE THEM YOURSELF

You do not have to invent or create a product to control the rights to it and manufacture it yourself. Often you can buy the mail order rights to certain products inexpensively. You then make them yourself at a cost lower than what the source would charge you for them.

To get the mail order rights, approach the patent or copyright owner directly. An individual or small firm will probably be open to talking with you, and you may be able to negotiate a deal. Larger corporations, as a rule, will not be interested and will not even talk to you. But there are exceptions.

If you are uncomfortable about negotiating such deals, ask your lawyer for pointers, or hire a lawyer to handle the negotiations for you.

c. BUY MERCHANDISE WHOLESALE AND RESELL IT TO CONSUMERS

You do not have to invent, own the rights to, or manufacture your own products. If you can buy goods from manufacturers or wholesalers at prices that allow you to mark up the items two to four times or more, you can sell them at a profit via mail order.

When you see an item you are excited about, contact the manufacturer. The manufacturer may deal with you directly or instead instruct you to buy through one of its wholesalers.

There are a number of wholesalers that specialize in selling merchandise to smaller mail order operators. Several of these are listed in Appendix 6.

1. Stocking inventory

If your mail order company offers merchandise from wholesalers, you will buy items in bulk and receive a deep discount off the retail price. When you are just starting out, get the minimum inventory the seller will allow you to carry. Avoid dealing with any company that requires you to maintain a large inventory. If the item doesn't sell, you could be stuck with the leftovers.

2. Consignment sales

An alternative to stocking inventory is consignment sales. In consignment selling, the manufacturer ships you a small supply of the item. You offer it for sale to your mail order customers. As you sell items, you send the manufacturer an agreed-on amount of money per sale. If the products do not sell, you can return all or some of them and owe nothing for those units returned. This eliminates your risk and allows you more flexibility in trying new items in your mail order product line.

3. Drop shipping

Some manufacturers, publishers, and wholesalers do not require mail order dealers to maintain any inventory. Instead, they will drop ship for you. In drop shipping, you advertise the item in your mailer, ad, or catalogue. When you get an order, you keep your cut of the money and send the product manufacturer its percentage of the money from the sale, along with a label addressed to your customer. The manufacturer affixes the label to a package and ships directly from its facility to your customer, but it looks like the product is coming from you because your label is on it.

d. BUY REMAINDERS, EXCESS INVENTORY, AND "DAMAGED" GOODS

When a publisher puts a book out of print, or a manufacturer discontinues an item, there may still be thousands of units left in inventory. Often, if the manufacturer can sell all or many of these items to one buyer, it will sell them at or below cost. This means you can pick them up cheaply.

Many mail order marketers buy inventories of out-of-print books or discontinued merchandise and sell them at a profit. Because you can buy these items for such a low cost, you can sell them at a discount off the retail price and still make a good profit.

Also, with clever promotional copy, you can turn the fact that the product is discontinued or out of print into a selling feature. An out-of-print book is a "rare manuscript, unavailable in bookstores or through book catalogues." A discontinued item is "a one-of-a-kind collector's item that, once sold out, will never be available again at any price." If it's a record that bombed in the record stores, you say, "Not one music aficionado in a thousand has heard the strains of these haunting melodies before." This kind of talk appeals to the mail order buyer, who is motivated by the exclusivity and rarity of the item.

A product that didn't do well in a retail store may become very successful if properly promoted via mail order. Most mail order operators are content to reap the profits as they sell thousands of remainder units, bought at deep discount, at full mail order price. If the product is spectacularly successful, you may want to acquire the rights and begin manufacturing or printing it yourself.

6

PRICING AND PRICE TESTING

What should you charge for your products? Common sense, interestingly enough, does not always produce the correct answer. One mail order entrepreneur found his ad generated more orders for a loose-leaf service at $297 than at $197! Finding the right price for your mail order products — the right price being the one that maximizes your profit — is an important part of your business.

a. DETERMINING THE OPTIMUM PRICE

The optimum price is the one that generates the most revenue. You can guess what this price will be, based on experience and what competitors are charging. The only way to precisely determine the optimum price is to price test.

The first step is to determine what prices you will test. Let's say you are selling a health newsletter to consumers. If you look around, you will see subscriptions for such newsletters range from $19 to $59 a year or more. So perhaps you will test $29, $39, and $49. If $49 wins, test $49 versus $59.

Your price is determined by several factors, including what the market will bear, your product costs, and what similar products are selling for.

"What the market will bear" refers to the amount of money people are willing to pay for your product. You can guess at this based on common sense and talking with potential buyers. But only price testing shows what this price actually is.

Your product cost determines the minimum price you can sell the product for and still make a profit. This is not the optimum price. Remember, for a front-end mail order product, the price should be at least three to four times your production and fulfillment costs, preferably higher. For a back-end product, the price should be at least twice your costs. Therefore, if your product costs $12.99 per unit to manufacture, and you think consumers won't pay more than $20, you will have a difficult time selling it via mail order since the profit margin is about $7 per unit (less than 40% of your costs).

Competition also affects pricing. You may think your health newsletter is unique and worth thousands of dollars a year because it will save the subscriber that much in hospital bills, illness, pain, and suffering. But if similar health newsletters are available for $49 a year, consumers will not want to pay $1,000 for yours.

1. How to price test inexpensively

How do you price test? It's easy. If you want to test three prices, send out 6,000 direct mail pieces — 2,000 for each of the three prices. You can key code of course (discussed in further detail in chapter 14), but you can also measure results just from the number of orders at each price. At a cost of $600 per thousand pieces in the mail, mailing the 6,000 pieces will cost you $3,600.

If you are running inquiry-generating ads, create two or three different order forms, one for each price you want to test. Make sure you fulfill orders evenly with the various price offers. For example, if you get 30 inquiries, fulfill 10 with the $19 order form, 10 with the $29 order form, and 10 with the $39 order form. Keep track of packages sent and response received.

2. Pricing in specialized versus general markets

We talked about competition, profit margin, and what the market will bear as factors in determining the price of mail order products. The audience you are selling to also has an effect on what you can charge.

As a rule, products aimed at a general consumer market are priced lower than specialized products aimed at specific markets. For instance, if you are selling to business opportunity seekers a book on how to get rich in mail order, you probably cannot charge more than $10 or $20, because information on this subject is available elsewhere.

On the other hand, if you write and sell a report for chiropractors called "Building Your $250,000 a Year Practice," you can charge more. In this case, this specialized audience has more money than general consumers, the profit return from the product is large compared with the purchase price, and you are offering highly specialized information targeted to the audience's specific interests and needs — information that is perceived as not available from other sources.

b. PRICING PSYCHOLOGY

Knowing what to charge for a product or service is one of the most difficult decisions marketers make. In mail order, however, we have an edge. We can try selling our products at different prices, measure the response to our ads and mailings, calculate the sales and profits at each price level, and determine the optimum price to charge.

1. The lowest price isn't always the best

Although you might think you would get more orders at the lowest price you could afford to charge, this is not always the case. It's true that people want to save money and get bargains. It's also true that, if you charge too little, customers might get the impression that your products are inferior. For this reason, sometimes you get more orders with a higher price. Many times, of course, the lower price wins.

Keep in mind that the price that generates the most orders is not always the most profitable. For example, let's say you have a product that costs $10 to make and you are testing two prices — $29 in ad A and $49 in ad B. The lower-priced offer, ad A, generates the most orders, with 100 people ordering the book for sales of $2,900.

Ad B does not generate as many orders; only 70 people order the book at the higher price of $49. But 70 orders times $49 per order is $3,430. So even though ad B generated 30% fewer orders, it produced $530 in more sales than ad A.

2. "Supermarket" versus even-number pricing

When setting the prices of mail order products, use "supermarket" pricing. This means you should charge $49, not $50. Or

$19.95 instead of $20. You don't always have to have a number that ends in 9, by the way. I once read an article advocating prices that end in 7, such as $29.97, instead of $29.95 or $29.99. Although the technique of supermarket pricing seems superficial, it does in fact work. People are more accepting of a $49.95 price tag than a $50 price tag. Price your mail order products accordingly.

3. Price points and barriers

A "price point" is a psychological barrier that stands in the way of the prospect going ahead with the purchase. For instance, $10 is a price point. If the price is $9 or $8 or $7, the price is not an obstacle. But prospects think harder about parting with their money as soon as you hit $10.

Other major price points are $20, $25, $30, $40, $50, $70, and $100. Always set your price slightly below the closest price point to what you were thinking of charging. For instance, if you are thinking of charging $102, go below the $100 price point and set the price at $99. You will most likely get more sales this way. If you want to get $102, state the price as $99 plus $3 shipping and handling.

c. OVERCOMING PRICE RESISTANCE

As we have discussed throughout this book, you need a mark-up of three, four, five, or more times the manufacturing cost to profitably sell a product via mail order. Therefore, it's tough to sell a low-priced product as a front-end direct mail offer. The only advantage of offering a lower-priced product is that there is not as much consumer price resistance. At low prices, the decision to order is more of an impulse buy, especially in mail order where customers

know they can always return items for refund (see section **1.** below).

With a high-priced product, you have a better profit margin and a much better chance of generating a profit from ads and direct mail. The only disadvantage is that an unusually high price can be a barrier to a sale, as the consumer spends a lot more time considering the purchase. There are several strategies to use to overcome price resistance.

1. Offer a money-back guarantee

One solution is to write your copy to imply that the person is not buying the product but merely "trying it risk free" for 30 days or whatever the terms of your money-back guarantee period are. Positioning the offer as a trial rather than as a sale can help overcome price resistance.

2. Offer a discount

Set the "list price" of your product slightly higher than the mail order price you actually want to charge. Then, in your mail order promotions, offer the product at a discount, which results in the price you actually want to charge.

For instance, if you sell an expensive software program and want to charge $295, say in your copy that the list price is $395, but if customers order now through this special mail order offer, they receive a $100 discount and pay the special low price of $295. Prospects perceive they are getting a mail order bargain, and this offer will generate more inquiries than just saying the price is $295.

Note: If you are operating in Canada, be sure to check any discount or free offers with your lawyer before running your promotion to ensure compliance with Canadian law.

3. Accept credit cards

Accepting credit card orders boosts response. The main reason is probably that it is convenient for the buyer. But I also think credit cards help overcome price resistance. When you write a check to a company for $50, you are acutely aware of how much money you are shelling out, and it seems like a lot. But when you use your credit card, the bill is "invisible" until you receive your credit card statement — after the fact. So for higher-priced offers — $50 and up — you should think about getting merchant status from MasterCard, Visa, and American Express (see chapter 2, section **g.**).

4. Offer easy payment plans

Another way to overcome price resistance for expensive mail order products is to bill the customer's credit card in installments. These payment plans allow you to write copy that creates the perception of a lower, more affordable price. After all, which sounds more affordable — "send $60" or "three easy payments of only $20 each"?

Look at ads from Franklin Mint, a mail order company that sells collectibles. These small collectibles are expensive — some are $40 to $50 or more. Franklin Mint advertises them at two, three, or four payments of only $17.50.

Rodale Press sells books by mail, many of which cost $25 to $29 or so. Because the customer may think that's a bit much to pay for a single book, Rodale offers a payment plan of three installments and emphasizes the per-installment price, rather than the total price, in its promotions.

5. Offer premiums

Offering premiums — free gifts — with an order can also help overcome price resistance. By offering multiple premiums, you give prospects the impression that they are getting a lot for their money, so they are less bothered by the price you are charging. One effective technique is to list all the premiums, give each a high list price, add up the total list price of the product and premiums, and then show how far below this total your asking price is.

6. Offer multicomponent products

Another way to create a high perceived value for your offer and therefore overcome price resistance is to describe to the buyer all the pieces and components of your product.

Take a look at the infomercials for Anthony Robbins, for "how to make money in real estate" courses, or for Don Dupree's money-making program. The information you are being offered is never packaged in a single book or manual, since people are unaccustomed to paying a premium price for just a book (they are trained from shopping in bookstores to perceive a single book as worth $10 to $25 retail).

Instead, for the selling price of $49 or $79 or whatever, you get a multicomponent package consisting of audiocassettes, manuals, a book or two, worksheets, and perhaps a short video or other component. You don't know the exact price of each of the individual elements, but since there are five or six components to the product, the price seems a bargain.

You may object that this is trickery and gimmickry, but it is not deceptive and it works. The way you describe your offer — the product, the premiums, the price, the guarantee, the payment terms — can have an enormous impact on response. Do not ignore these facts when creating your own offers.

7

MAKING MONEY WITH CLASSIFIED ADS

The least expensive way to start in mail order is with small classified ads. Actually, these ads generate a greater return on investment than any other medium, including full-page ads. With a winning classified ad and strong inquiry fulfillment kit (see chapter 8), you have the foundation for a profitable home-based mail order business.

a. HOW CLASSIFIED ADS WORK

Classified advertising is two-step direct marketing. In step one, you run a small classified ad to generate an inquiry, which is a request for more information about your product.

In step two, when people inquire, you send out an inquiry fulfillment kit, which is a sales package promoting your product. The inquiry fulfillment kit, described in chapter 8, consists of an outer envelope, sales letter, circular or brochure, order form, and reply envelope. A successful inquiry fulfillment kit should convert 10% to 15% of the inquiries to orders. Some inquiry fulfillment kits have achieved conversion rates as high as 20% to 30%, or even a little higher.

You should not ask for an order directly from a classified ad. It usually won't work. There is not enough copy in a classified ad to make the complete sale.

The way to measure classified ad response is to count the inquiries and divide the cost of the ad by the number of inquiries to determine the cost per inquiry. For instance, if it costs you $100 to run a classified ad and you get 100 inquiries, your cost per inquiry is $1. A successful classified ad will generate inquiries at a cost of between 50¢ and $2 per inquiry.

b. HOW TO WRITE AN EFFECTIVE CLASSIFIED AD

Bernard Lyons, a mail order expert, says that classified ads must follow the AIDA principle, meaning they must —

(a) get **Attention**,

(b) generate **Interest**,

(c) create **Desire** for the product, and

(d) ask for **Action**.

According to Lyons, sales appeals that work in classified mail order advertising include promises that the customer will obtain love, money, health, popularity, success, leisure, security, self-confidence, better appearance, self-improvement, pride of accomplishment, prestige, pride of ownership, or comfort; will receive entertainment; will save time; will eliminate worry and fear; will satisfy curiosity, self-expression, or creativity; or will avoid work or risk.

Lyons says the six most effective words and phrases to use in your classified ads are —

- free,
- new,
- amazing,
- now,
- how to, and
- easy.

To this list I add —

- discover,
- method,
- plan,
- reveals,
- show,
- simple,
- startling,
- advanced,
- improved, and
- you.

One of my most successful mail order ads, run continuously for many years in *Writer's Digest*, reads as follows:

MAKE $85,000/YEAR writing ads, brochures, promotional materials for local/national client. Free details: CTC, 22 E. Quackenbush, Dept. WD, Dumont, NJ 07628.

Here are some other examples of how to write classified mail order ads:

EXTRA CASH. 12 ways to make money at home. Free details ...

MAIL ORDER MILLIONAIRE reveals money-making secrets. FREE 1-hour cassette ...

SELL NEW BOOK by mail! 400% profit! Free dealer information ...

GROW earthworms at home for profit ...

CARNIVOROUS AND WOODLAND terrarium plants. Send for FREE catalogue ...

ANCESTOR HUNTING? Trace your family roots the easy way. Details free ...

1. Why shorter is better

The measure of a successful classified ad is the cost per inquiry. Therefore, if you can get your message across in fewer words, you pay less for the ad and, as a result, lower your cost per inquiry.

Make your classifieds as short and pithy as possible. Here are some tips for reducing your word count:

(a) **Be concise.** Use the minimum number of words needed to communicate your idea. For example, instead of "Earn $500 a Day in Your Own

Home-Based Business," write "Work at Home — $500/Day!"

(b) **Minimize your address.** You pay the publication for every word in your classified, including your address. Therefore, instead of "22 E. Quackenbush Avenue," I write "22 E. Quackenbush." The mail will still be delivered, and I will save one word. This can add up to significant savings for ads run frequently in multiple publications.

(c) **Use phrases and sentence fragments rather than full sentences.**

(d) **Remember your objective.** You are asking only for an inquiry, not for an order. You don't need a lot of copy, since all you are asking the reader to do is send for free information.

(e) **Use combination words, hyphenated words, and slash constructions.** For instance, instead of "GROW EARTH WORMS," which is three words, write "GROW EARTHWORMS," which counts as two words, saving you a word.

2. What to offer in your classified ad

The best way to generate a response is to ask for an inquiry, rather than an order. This is done by putting a phrase such as "free details," "free information," "free catalogue," or similar phrase, followed by a colon and your address (e.g., free details: Box 54, Canuga, TN 44566).

3. Should you charge for your information?

Some mail order advertisers ask the prospect to pay for the information, either by sending a small amount of money (25¢, 50¢, $1, and $2 are typical) or by sending a self-addressed envelope with the postage already on it.

The theory is that asking for postage or a nominal payment brings you a more qualified lead and therefore results in a higher percentage of leads converted to sales. My experience is that it doesn't pay to charge for your information kit, since doing so dramatically cuts down on the number of leads you will receive.

Whenever you offer information to generate an inquiry, I believe it's best to make it free. The exception might be if you are offering a very expensive and elaborate catalogue, for which you charge $1 or $2 to cover your costs.

4. Key code your ad

Chapter 14 tells you how to key code all your promotions, so you can track which ad or mailing brought in each inquiry or order. In your classified ads, put the key code in the address. For instance, in my ad "MAKE $85,000/YEAR WRITING," the key code "WD" refers to *Writer's Digest* magazine. Since the ad runs every month, I don't bother adding a code number to track the month. If you wanted to do so, you could. For example, "Dept. WD-10" would mean *Writer's Digest* magazine, October issue (the tenth month of the year). Keep track of the key code on each inquiry, and record the information using the form in Worksheet #1.

c. WHEN IS A CLASSIFIED AD PROFITABLE?

We have already discussed the two key measurements of two-step classified advertising: the cost per inquiry and the percentage of inquiries converted to orders.

The bottom line is this: did the sales the ad generated exceed the cost of the ad space? If they did, it was profitable. If they didn't, the ad isn't working, and a new ad should be tested.

To succeed in mail order, you must quickly determine whether a particular ad or mailing is making money so you can roll it out if it's a winner — and stop using it if it's unprofitable. Worksheet #1 is a form you can use to track response to and sales from your mail order promotions on a daily and monthly basis (Sample #2 shows how to use this form). It will tell you immediately which is pulling best. You can also, at a glance, compare the cost of the ad space with the total sales generated. My goal is to generate sales of at least twice what the ad space costs. Your objectives may be different.

Photocopy this form and keep copies in a three-ring binder labeled "Mail Order Sales." Every ad or mailing gets its own monthly sheet. With 12 tabs, divide the binder into months. Alternatively, you can keep these records on your computer (see chapter 2, section **f.1.**) using any of the software programs listed in Appendix 3. Keeping monthly records shows you if your response rates vary depending on the time of year. It also helps you calculate sales by quarter for purposes of paying sales tax.

d. WHERE TO PLACE CLASSIFIED ADS

Place your classified ads in publications that have mail order classified ad sections. Appendix 7 lists some of the publications known to be effective for mail order advertising. Most of these have classified ad sections.

Contact the magazines that interest you and ask for their media kits, which include details on circulation, advertising rates, and readership, and a sample issue of the publication. Ask if the publisher will send several sample issues.

Look at the classified ad sections in the publications. Are the ads for products similar to yours? This is a good sign. See if these ads repeat from issue to issue. The advertisers would not repeat them unless the ads were working. If this publication is working for their offers, it can work for yours too.

Classified ad sections are divided by various headings. Place your ad under the appropriate heading. If you don't see an appropriate heading, call the magazine and ask if it will create one for you.

If you sell information by mail, avoid putting your classified under the heading "Books and Booklets." This will reduce orders. Instead, put the ad under a heading related to the subject matter. For example, if you are selling a book on how to make money cleaning chimneys, place the ad under "Business opportunities."

e. TESTING NEW PUBLICATIONS

You can test a classified ad by running it just one time in a publication. The problem is, most magazines, and even weekly newspapers, have long lead times — several weeks or more — for placing classified ads. If you place the ad to run one time only and the ad pulls well, you then must wait several weeks or months until you can get it in the publication again.

In a weekly newspaper or magazine, I test a classified ad by running it for one month — four consecutive issues. For a monthly publication, I test it for three

WORKSHEET #1
RESPONSE TRACKING FORM

Month_____Year_____

Ad or mailing_____Key code_____

Product_____Offer_____

Total cost_____Total sales_____

	Day	# Inquiries	Total inquiries to date	Day's sales	Total sales to date
1					
2					
3					
4					
5					
6					
7					
8					
9					
10					
11					
12					
13					
14					
15					
16					
17					
18					
19					
20					
21					
22					
23					

	Day	# Inquiries	Total inquiries to date	Day's sales	Total sales to date
24					
25					
26					
27					
28					
29					
30					
31					

months — three consecutive issues. If the first insertion is profitable, I will probably extend the insertion order for several months so the ad runs continuously with no interruption.

f. LONGEVITY AND RESPONSE CURVE OF CLASSIFIED ADS

With a full-page ad, you usually get the greatest number of orders the first time the ad runs in the magazine. Response declines with each additional insertion; at the point where the ad is not going to be profitable in its next insertion, you pull it and try another ad.

The reason for this response pattern is that the first time the ad runs, it skims the cream of the prospects, getting orders from those most likely to buy. Obviously, those who buy from the first insertion of the ad will not buy when it runs again. Therefore, each time the ad runs it reaches a smaller and smaller audience of potential new buyers.

While response to full-page mail order ads declines with each insertion, the response to a classified ad can remain steady for many insertions. Indeed, some mail order operators (and I am one of them) have run the same classified ad monthly in the same magazine for years at a time, with no decline in response. Response sometimes increases during the first 12 months the ad is run, as people see the ad over and over again and eventually become curious enough to respond.

Some people who responded once, received your sales literature, and didn't buy, may respond several times — and get your literature several times — before they eventually break down and buy. Also, each issue reaches a number of new subscribers via subscriptions and newsstand circulation, so the total audience for a classified remains fairly constant.

SAMPLE #2
RESPONSE TRACKING FORM

Month___*January*___ Year___*97*___
Ad or mailing___*Secrets*___ Key code_____
Product_____ Offer_____
Total cost_____ Total sales_____

	Day	# Inquiries	Total inquiries to date	Day's sales	Total sales to date
1					
2	2	ll			
3					
4	4	HH HH HH l			
5					
6					
7					
8	8	HH			
9	9				
10	10	HH HH HH HH llll			
11	11				
12	12	HH ll		51 =	
13	13	HH lll			
14					
15					
16	16	HH HH llll			
17	17	HH HH l		49 =	
18	18			51 =	
19					
20	20			51 =	
21					
22	22	HH lll			
23	23			51	

8

CREATING YOUR INQUIRY FULFILLMENT PACKAGE

In addition to receiving direct orders with payment enclosed, you will get many inquiries from people requesting more information about your product. You need a strong inquiry fulfillment package to convert these leads to sales. There are certain elements that must be included in this package:

(a) Outer envelope

(b) Sales letter

(c) Circular

(d) Order form

(e) Reply envelope

An inquiry fulfillment package sent to someone who requests more information on your product must be as powerful and persuasive as a direct mail package mailed cold to a list of rented prospects. Too many mail order marketers respond to inquiries by stuffing a bunch of flyers or brochures in the mail. The problem with that approach is that a lead is not a sale. You spend money to generate the inquiry; your business will not be profitable unless you can convert many of those inquiries to orders. That's accomplished only with a strong inquiry fulfillment package.

a. OUTER ENVELOPE

The inquiry fulfillment package is sent in a #10 envelope or, if your brochures are full size, a 9-by-12-inch envelope. Type the customer's name and address directly on the #10 envelope. Use labels for the 9-by-12-inch envelope.

Mail the inquiry fulfillment materials first class. On the outer envelope, imprint or stamp a notice that tells prospects this is material they sent for. "HERE IS THE INFORMATION YOU REQUESTED" is hand-stamped on my envelopes in red ink. Don't use a creative teaser as you would in unsolicited direct mail; the prospect will treat your package as advertising mail, not as information he or she asked for.

b. SALES LETTER

A strong sales letter can make the difference between an inquiry fulfillment package that is mediocre and one that is highly profitable. The sales letter performs the following functions:

(a) **Thanks prospects for their inquiries.** Remind them that they requested the information enclosed — you did not send it to them unsolicited.

(b) **Talks about the reason why the prospect requested the information.** If your ad says, "Earn $200 a Day as a Chimney Sweep," remind prospects that you can help them achieve their financial goals and earn $200 a day.

(c) **Positions the product you are selling as the solution to their needs.** For the chimney sweep ad, tell prospects that your product (probably a course on how to get set up in a chimney cleaning business) will show them how to start and run a highly successful part- or full-time business cleaning chimneys.

(d) **Talks about the benefits of your product — how it will help them earn more money, save time, look better, be healthier, and so on.** Help prospects visualize what life will be like when they have these benefits. For instance, if you are going to help them make a lot of money, ask how they'd like it if they were out of debt and could quit their day job, take luxury vacations, own expensive cars, and so on.

(e) **Talks about the great things your product offers.** Be specific. You must convince prospects that your product can deliver the benefits you promise and that your product is superior to other alternatives they might purchase to achieve their goal.

(f) **Eliminates the risk of buying.** Offer your product on a money-back guarantee basis. Tell your customers that if they are not satisfied, they may return the product within 30 or 60 or 90 days and you will refund their money in full.

(g) **Asks for the order.** Tell them what to do next to place their order.

Sample #3 shows a sales letter I send to people who respond to my classified ads in *Writer's Digest* (the classified ad reprinted in chapter 7 with the headline "MAKE $85,000 A YEAR"). People who respond get this letter, a flyer that describes the book and has a tear-off order form, and a reply envelope. The letter typically converts 15% to 30% of inquiries to sales, depending on which publication the inquiries came from.

c. CIRCULAR

In addition to the letter, your inquiry fulfillment package can have a flyer, circular, brochure, or other literature. This circular further elaborates on the features and benefits of your product and may contain illustrations or photos that show what the product looks like, what elements are included, how it works, how it is used, and the benefits people get from using it (for instance, if your product is a stomach exerciser, you would show pictures of people with flat, hard stomachs).

There is a saying in mail order: "The letter sells; the brochure tells." The letter is the main persuasive component of the package. The circular amplifies or expands on points made in the letter, or illustrates them to make them clear.

The circular need not be printed in four colors. One or two colors is fine. Most mail order circulars are black ink on a colored paper stock, such as green, blue, or yellow. You can produce them on your desktop computer and reprint them at a local copy shop or offset printer.

Thanks for your request —
here's the information you asked
me to send you . . .

HERE'S HOW I MADE $190,296 BY STAYING HOME AND WRITING

Dear Writer:

The writing life is a great life. I love staying home, avoiding the rat race, and getting paid good money to sit at my beloved 486 computer — thinking, reading, and writing for my clients.

Now, I want to show you <u>how to stay home writing while earning $500 a day — or $50,000 to $76,000 to $100,000 a YEAR or more.</u>

What's the secret? I call it . . .

HIGH-PROFIT WRITING

<u>High-Profit Writing</u> is a different type of writing. You don't usually read about it in the writer's magazines, or hear about it on TV or radio talk shows.

It doesn't have anything to do with writing books or magazine articles (although I've written 18 books and more than 100 articles in my spare time).

<u>Most</u> writers hope to earn fame and fortune through books and articles. But it rarely works out. The pay scales are LOW (except for a handful of superstars). And the field is too crowded.

If you've ever submitted a manuscript or query letter, you know what I'm talking about.

Instead, <u>High-Profit Writing</u> deals with the field of commercial writing: creating ads, brochures, and promotional materials for national corporations . . . local businesses . . . entrepreneurs . . . nonprofits . . . and other organizations and institutions that need written materials to sell their products, educate their audiences, raise funds, or enhance their public image.

HOW MUCH MONEY CAN YOU MAKE IN <u>HIGH-PROFIT WRITING</u>?

The profits are so huge in this business that to the beginner, they may seem astounding.

For example, I was recently paid $4,500 by one client to write a direct mail package. Another client paid me $9,000 to write a more complex mailing consisting of a sales letter, brochure, and order form.

One bank hired me to write two brochures for two different divisions. The check they sent me was for $5,760. And, although my income is well into six figures (last year I grossed $190,296), there are others earning even more:

**Eugene Schwartz, a well-known direct mail writer, gets $24,000 (yes, $24,000) to write a sales package.

**Writer Richard Armstrong, who is also an author and actor, charges $2,500 for a 20-minute speech.

**One woman who moonlights 17 hours a week earned $30,000 in nine months using my methods.

**I recently wrote four brochures in four weeks for one client. My fee? $18,400. That same month, another client hired me to write six simple "product data sheets" for a fee of $11,600.

And best of all, there is no querying. No outlines. No proposals to editors. No library research or "journalistic" reporting involved.

Instead, the clients come to YOU with assignments. You receive an advance retainer check and a contract. You are provided with ALL the research material and background you need. All you do is WRITE.

You are paid for your ideas and creativity — not your legwork. And if you are asked for advice, you can charge a consulting fee of <u>$50 to $400 an hour</u>. (My friend Dr. Andrew Linick gets his fee up front and is booked nine months in advance.) You don't give your ideas away for free, as magazine editors expect you to do.

NOW YOU CAN MAKE BIG MONEY THROUGH FREELANCE WRITING STARTING TODAY

After loving this business for nine years, I realized that (a) there is more than enough work to go around and (b) for that reason, why not help other writers and share the wealth?

To make it easy for you, I sat down and wrote a complete PLAN, sharing with you exactly what is involved in the <u>High-Profit Writing</u> business.

You'll discover what you have to do — step by step — to break in, get started, and make a lot of money writing ads. Brochures. Booklets. Direct mail letters. Press releases. Audio-visual scripts. Speeches. Manuals. Articles. Company newsletters. And other materials for local and national clients.

Because my copyrighted plan has never been available to writers until now, I call it "SECRETS OF A FREELANCE WRITER."

My plan shows you EVERYTHING you need to succeed. Nothing is **left out**. For the first time, ALL the secrets of the high-paid commercial writers are revealed in full detail.

HERE'S JUST A SAMPLING OF THE SECRETS REVEALED IN "SECRETS OF A FREELANCE WRITER":

- The best clients for freelance writers — where to find them; how to get them to hire you.

- How to earn $1,000 to $3,000 per assignment "ghostwriting" articles and speeches for busy executives.

- Which freelance assignments pay best? TIP: Not all pay equally well. I tell you which are lucrative and which are losers.

- The seven reasons why potential clients need your services <u>even though they already have an ad agency, staff writers, or use other freelancers</u>.

- How to get paid big money from local businesses for your ideas and advice.

- How to write a sales letter that brings you two to ten new potential clients (companies who want to hire you) for every 100 letters you mail.

READERS OF "SECRETS OF A FREELANCE WRITER" SAY IT BEST

"Your books have been a great inspiration to me. In two years, I have gone from zero customers, zero prospects, zero ad-agency experience, and zero income to working with <u>Fortune</u> 600 companies like Hewlett-Packard, earning $85,000+ per year and quickly closing in on a six figure income. Thanks."
Steve Edwards, Carlsbad, CA

"Reading 'SECRETS OF A FREELANCE WRITER,' particularly the tips on contracts, saved me at least $10,000 in six months."
Catherine Gonick, Jersey City, NJ

"With Bob's practical ideas and clear advice, I've been able to land jobs I would never have thought of before and establish myself as a highly successful full-time professional freelance writer."
Joe Vitale, Houston, TX

TRY "SECRETS OF A FREELANCE WRITER" FOR 90 DAYS RISK-FREE

To order "SECRETS OF A FREELANCE WRITER," just fill in the coupon portion of the enclosed pink circular and mail it to me with your check or money order.

I'll rush the program to you (over 270 pages of instruction plus six audiocassettes) as soon as I hear from you. If you are not 100% delighted with my material, simply return it within 90 days for a full, prompt refund no questions asked.

I can't think of a fairer . . . or easier . . . way for you to sample my High-Profit Writing techniques without risking a penny.

As I said at the beginning: the writing life is a great life especially if you are getting paid handsomely to sit home and do it. Why not enjoy the good life now instead of later?

Send for my instructions and get started today. There is no risk or obligation of any kind. And your satisfaction is guaranteed. You can't lose.

Yours for success,
Bob Bly, The High-Profit Writer

PS: Wondering how much to charge clients for an article, press release, brochure, booklet, ad, newsletter, or sales letter? A complete and up-to-date table of fees appears on page 26 of "SECRETS OF A FREELANCE WRITER." Consult this fee schedule before quoting your fee to a prospective client to make sure your price is in line with what the client expects to pay
Bob Bly / 22 E. Quackenbush Avenue / Dumont, NJ 07628 /
(201) 385-1220

d. ORDER FORM

Always include an order form with your inquiry fulfillment package. The order form can be a separate piece of paper or it can be part of the circular or letter.

The order form should have space for customers to fill in their shipping information, tell you what they are ordering, and indicate their method of payment. It is also a good idea to restate your guarantee right on the order form. Sample #4 shows an order form for my "Secrets of a Freelance Writer" mailing.

e. REPLY ENVELOPE

You should also enclose a reply envelope in your inquiry fulfillment kit. Prospects use the reply envelope to mail back the order form with their credit card information or check.

You can use a plain envelope and require the prospect to provide postage, or you can use a business reply envelope. With business reply mail, you — not the customer — pay the cost of postage for any envelope returned to you. Your local post office will provide you with complete information on how business reply mail works and how your printer must prepare your business reply envelopes. It is not at all complicated.

Will you get more orders by using business reply envelopes instead of plain envelopes? This is something you can test for yourself. When you get a batch of inquiries, key code the order forms (as you did your ads, and discussed further in chapter 14) and mail half in business reply envelopes, half in regular envelopes. Then measure the response.

If you use a plain envelope that requires the customer to affix postage, put a box that says "Place Stamp Here" in the upper right-hand corner of the front of the envelope.

If you want to pay postage, use a business reply permit. Do not affix postage stamps to reply envelopes. If you do, you are paying the postage on every envelope, whether it is returned or not. Considering that around 98 out of 100 reply envelopes you mail with inquiry fulfillment kits will not be returned, it is a foolish waste of money to affix postage stamps. With business reply envelopes, you pay postage only on those envelopes returned to you.

f. ADDITIONAL ELEMENTS (OPTIONAL)

Your inquiry fulfillment package is flexible in format. You can add additional elements as you wish. The three most popular inserts are the lift letter, the buck slip, and the "freemium."

1. Lift letter

The lift letter is a second, smaller letter that is sent in addition to the main letter. It is usually one-page long and printed on Monarch (five-by-seven inch) paper rather than on full-size paper. The lift note can be used to restate the offer, stress the guarantee, or emphasize benefits. The lift letter explains and highlights the offer already made in the other package elements; it does not add new information or make additional offers not covered in the other elements.

2. Buck slip

A buck slip is a small slip of paper, usually four-by-nine inches in size, enclosed with the other elements of the inquiry fulfillment package. The buck slip is typically

SAMPLE #4
ORDER FORM

Here's what Writer's Digest Book Club says about *Secrets of a Freelance Writer*

(For comments from satisfied customers, see reverse side...)

To order your copy, mail this handy coupon today.

Secrets of a Freelance Writer:
How to Make $85,000 a Year
6 audio cassettes + 272-page book

If you've quietly resigned yourself to the notion that writing is incompatible with good pay, then the pledge Robert Bly makes in his preface ought to wake you up:

"You'll be in a position to earn big money from your writing, whenever you need it."

No small promise, this. Yet Bly will not only convince you it's attainable, he'll *show* you exactly how to go about it. And there's only one prerequisite: you must give up romantic notions of striking it rich with your first novel in favor of a hard-nosed approach to what Bly calls "commercial" writing. This is a different animal altogether, one that requires you to apply your wordsmithing skills to meet the writing needs of clients. It is a *business* approach to writing, and a profitable one. Bly knows; he's done it.

Best of all, you don't have to give up writing that novel, or play. Bly predicts that if you work at commercial freelancing part time— practicing his principles— you can earn enough to support your novel (play/ poetry) "habit." Wouldn't it be nice to have those sales as gravy?

Bly defines commercial writing as creating just about any kind of printed or audiovisual material a client might need in promoting a product, service, or idea. It runs the gamut from writing a press release to creating a direct mail package to composing an audiovisual or radio commercial script. For the raw beginner in each of the many types of such "collaterals"—or the pro in one area who wants to branch out—Bly offers definitions, outlines goals (to get an order/make a sale/promote an image to the public), and gives solid how-to information as well as suggestions for further reading. And he gives guidelines for fees—his own as well as a range within which yours might fit.

Bly gives you the wherewithal to *become* an expert on writing PR "backgrounders" or business-to-business print ads, even if you've never tried your hand at it. But perhaps the greatest strength of *Secrets of a Freelance Writer* lies in telling you where, and how, to get the business in the first place.

For Bly, this includes friendly, candid advice on how to do your *own* direct mail promotion (complete with response card for those who want your list of fees, etc.), how to use referrals and solicit testimonials, how and where to place ads for your services, and much more. Equally important, he tackles other important business matters: how to negotiate fees and assure payment, how to collect unpaid bills, how to handle "extra" revisions, etc.

Bly even hands you materials you can pick up and use, such as sales letters on his own writing business, verbatim. Why would he cheerfully offer to let you steal his hard work—and perhaps assignments as well? Simple. Dedication to the proposition that "writing is a professional service worth the fees that other professionals command." *Secrets of a Freelance Writer* aims to generate professionalism and promote a collective consciousness-raising. One freelancer who completes an assignment shoddily —*or* completes it well but charges too little— hurts the whole field, Bly observes. In the absence of a union, his book is the next best bet.

❑ **YES,** I'd like to make $100,000 a year or more as a freelance writer. Please send me _____ copies of *Secrets of a Freelance Writer*, including the 6 audio cassettes + FREE 272-page book, at $49.00 each (no charge for postage & handling). I understand that if I am not 100% delighted with this material, I may return it within 90 days and you will refund my money in full—no questions asked.

On that basis, here is my check for $_____ (payable to "Bob Bly").

Name _____ Address _____ _____

City _____ State_____ Zip _____

Please allow 2–4 weeks for delivery. NJ residents: Add 6% sales tax ($2.94 per copy) when ordering.
Canadian residents: Add $2 (two U.S. dollars).

❑ Please rush my materials. I've enclosed an extra $2 for first-class delivery.

MAIL TO: Bob Bly, 22 E. Quackenbush Avenue, Dumont, NJ 07628

used to highlight and show any premiums, which are free gifts customers receive when they order the main product.

3. "Freemium"

A "freemium" is a free gift enclosed with the inquiry fulfillment package. For instance, if you are selling a diet product, you can print some common foods and their calorie count on a small card and include this as a gift with the inquiry fulfillment materials. The purpose of the freemium is to get attention, get the prospect involved with the mailing, and demonstrate the value of the products you sell.

I was once asked to write a direct mail package to sell a popular science book on the topic of volcanoes and earthquakes. Among other things, the book contained instructions for making a simple model of a working volcano that would actually erupt! We reprinted these instructions on a sheet of paper, inserted them into the package as a freemium, and promoted it on the outer envelope with the intriguing teaser, "FREE volcano inside!"

9

MOVING UP TO FULL-PAGE ADS

The full-page ad is the quickest way to mail order riches. Unfortunately, it is also fraught with risk.

Since full-page ads are so much bigger than classifieds, they can potentially generate much more readership and response. This means you can potentially make thousands (or even tens of thousands) of dollars in sales and profits with a single insertion. You have to run a classified ad continuously over time to generate a large volume of sales, and the sales take place over a prolonged period, not all at once.

On the other hand, large ads are more risky. If the ad bombs, you can lose part or even all the money you invested running it. A full-page ad can cost you from $2,000 to $10,000 or more to run one time in one publication, depending on the magazine or newspaper you select. Classified ads can be run for $50 to $100 per insertion.

If your classified ad fails to pull orders, you have lost only a little money and can afford to try different ads until one works. Most of us, however, would be wiped out or at least hurt substantially by a $10,000 ad that pulls no orders. Make the move to full-page ads only if and when you can afford it.

a. FROM CLASSIFIED TO FRACTIONAL TO FULL-PAGE ADS

If you are currently a classified advertiser, there is no need to make the gigantic leap from tiny classified to full-page display ad all at once. Step up your ad size gradually. Instead of a classified, try a small one- or two-inch classified display ad, a quarter or a third or a sixth of a page in a magazine, or five to six column inches in a newspaper. If the bigger ads pull and are profitable, keep expanding the size. If they are not, keep testing at the smaller sizes until you find an ad that works. Then rewrite and expand to the next size up.

When should you take the plunge and try a full-page ad? It's up to you, but here's my advice: run your full-page ad using only "risk capital." This is money that, if you lost it all, wouldn't have a negative impact on your life psychologically or economically. In other words, don't gamble money on a full-page ad until and unless you can afford to lose it, because people do lose money on ads — all the time.

Some mail order entrepreneurs make the mistake of running a full-page ad as soon as they have enough money to do so.

Then, when it bombs, they have no capital left and cannot continue. If you are limited in capital, it's better to run smaller ads and build your mail order business slowly. You can afford to absorb failures and keep going until you hit on a winner. If every penny you have goes to paying for a full-page ad, you have only one shot to succeed and the odds are against you.

b. BUYING AD SPACE BELOW RATE CARD PRICING

Since the profit from mail order ads is determined by the ratio of sales generated to the cost of advertising, you have a better chance of making a profit if you can pay less money for an ad. There are several ways to do this:

(a) **P/I (per inquiry) deals.** In a P/I deal, you negotiate the following arrangement with the publication: the publication does not charge you to run the ad, but it receives 50% of the sales the ad generates. Although you give up more profit if the ad is successful, you minimize your up-front risk. Once a popular form of advertising, P/I is more difficult to arrange today, as fewer publishers are willing to risk it. But it doesn't hurt to ask.

(b) **Make good.** The term "make good" means the publisher reruns the ad for free if there is a problem with the first insertion. A variation on the make good is an alternative to the pure P/I deal. In this situation, you and the publisher agree that you will pay the regular rate to run your ad one time. However, if you do not make enough sales to cover the cost of the ad space on the first insertion, the publisher will give you a second insertion free or at a deep discount. Publishers with new magazines or who are having difficulty selling space during a particular month may be agreeable to this deal.

(c) **Remnant space.** Publishers must print a certain number of pages each issue. Sometimes the magazine's layout is such that, for a given month, there are leftover pages with nothing to put on them. This is known as remnant space, and publishers will sometimes sell it at a discount of up to 50% off their regular rates. Usually you can get remnant space only by prearranging such a deal with the publisher. You supply your ad film or a mechanical and instruct the publisher to run it, for an agreed-on discount, whenever there is remnant space. The advantage is you get the ad space at deep discount. The disadvantage is you never know when your ad is going to run.

(d) **Media buying services.** There are several large agencies that specialize in buying mail order ad space and reselling it to mail order advertisers. Because these companies buy huge volumes of space, they get major discounts from the publishers. They pass some of the discount on to you in the form of savings and keep the rest as their profit. A couple of these firms are listed in Appendix 7.

(e) **In-house agency discounts.** How do ad agencies make their money? Part of it has traditionally come from commissions on the space ads they place for clients. For instance, if an ad costs $10,000 to run, the magazine will give the agency a 15% discount, charging it only $8,500. You pay $10,000 to the agency, the agency pays the magazine $8,500, and it keeps $1,500 as its commission. This is a traditional and accepted practice. Years ago, agency discounts were given only to bona fide ad agencies. Today, however, many publications give agency discounts to practically anyone. If you place an ad yourself, using the insertion order form in Worksheet #2, you can often get the publication to give you the agency commission. The result is a savings of 15% on the ads you run — a substantial amount of money. (When copying the form, insert your own company name and address at the top, as in Sample #5.) Many publishers will give you an additional discount, typically 2%, if you enclose payment with the insertion order.

(f) **Run in the smaller publications in a particular field.** If you are going to test ads in a particular type of publication, such as supermarket tabloids, the ones with the smaller circulations will be less expensive to test. If your budget is limited, you may want to run in the magazine that charges $5,000 for an ad and has a circulation of 200,000, rather than in the magazine that has a circulation of 625,000 but charges $14,980 for a full-page ad. If the ad in the smaller circulation magazine is profitable, you can then test it in more expensive magazines with larger circulations. **Note:** Don't advertise in magazines with too few readers to produce mail order sales.

Mail order ads should usually be run only in publications with a circulation of 100,000 or more.

c. WHAT SHOULD YOU OFFER IN AN AD?

Should you encourage people to respond to your ad with an order for your product or with a request for more information? The answer depends on the value of your product.

If your product sells for $10 to $50, you can use a full-page ad to generate direct mail orders. That is, people read the ad and order the product directly from the ad.

If your product sells for several hundred dollars, you may want to use full-page ads to generate inquiries. You respond to these inquiries by mailing your inquiry fulfillment kit as described in chapter 8.

If your product is in the $50 to $300 price range, you can experiment with both inquiry- and order-generating ads until you determine which works best.

d. TIPS FOR WRITING EFFECTIVE MAIL ORDER ADS

Here are some techniques, methods, and principles that can help improve the odds that the next ad you create will be a winner — one that generates the immediate sales results you desire.

1. Advertise the right product for the right audience

The first step is to make sure you are advertising a product that is potentially useful to the people reading your advertisement. This seems to be a simple and obvious rule, yet many people believe that a great ad can sell anything to anyone. They are wrong.

WORKSHEET #2
ADVERTISING INSERTION ORDER

ADVERTISING INSERTION ORDER

From:_____

Date:_____

Advertiser:_____

Product:_____

To:_____

Publication in which ad is to run:_____

Date of insertion:_____

Size of ad:_____

Instructions:_____

Rate:_____

Less frequency discount_____%

Less agency commission_____% on gross

Less cash discount_____% on net

Net amount on this insertion order:_____

Insertion order placed by:_____

SAMPLE #5
ADVERTISING INSERTION ORDER

ADVERTISING INSERTION ORDER

From: _Bob Bly Advertising_

Date: _June 7, 1997_

Advertiser: _Writer's Profit Catalog_

Product: _"Secrets of a Freelance Writer!_

To: _Kate Jones, Ad Manager_

Publication in which ad is to run: _Writer's News_

Date of insertion: _September, 1997 issue_

Size of ad: _Full page_

Instructions: _Right-hand page — front of book_

Rate: _$2,000_

Less frequency discount _—_ %

Less agency commission _15_ % on gross

Less cash discount _—_ % on net

Net amount on this insertion order: _$1,700_

Insertion order placed by: _Bob Bly_

"Copy cannot create desire for a product," Eugene Schwartz writes in his book *Breakthrough Advertising*. "It can only focus already-existing desires onto a particular product. The copywriter's task is not to create this mass desire, but to channel and direct it."

For example, no advertisement, no matter how powerfully written, will convince the vegetarian to have a steak dinner at your new restaurant. But your ad, if persuasively worded, might entice him or her to try your salad bar.

Charles Inlander of the People's Medical Society is an expert at finding the right product for the right audience. His ad — headlined "Do you recognize the seven early warning signs of high blood pressure?" — sold more than 20,000 copies of a $4.95 book on blood pressure when it ran approximately ten times in *Prevention Magazine* over a three-year period.

"First, you select your topic," says Inlander, explaining the secret of his advertising success, "then you must find the right place to advertise. It's important to pinpoint a magazine whose readers are the right prospects for what you are selling." In other words, the right audience for the right product.

The late copywriter Paul Bringe gives this rule for selecting advertising media: "Fish where the fish are biting." Check the publications where you're thinking of running an ad. If there are ads for similar products and these ads are run repeatedly, that's a good sign. The publication must be working or these advertisers would not be spending their money to run the ads over and over again.

If a publication does not contain ads for offers similar to yours, you should hesitate to advertise there, even if the publication seems to reach the right audience. If the publication worked for your type of offer, other ads with similar offers would already be running there. Their absence suggests mail order companies tried the publication once and found it wanting. Proceed with caution.

Who are your prospects? PC users? Runners? Gardeners? Mothers? Are they likely to read the magazine you are considering for your advertisement? If not, you will have a difficult time. The right product for the audience might sell even if the ad is mediocre. The wrong product, aimed at the wrong group, will not sell even if the ad is dynamite.

If you advertise in publications where only a small percentage of the readers are prospects, you will be paying to reach too many people who are not potential buyers, and the ad will not pay off. The more targeted the publication is to your audience, the better your chances for success.

2. Use an attention-getting headline

Next to selecting subject matter and placing your ad in the proper publication, the headline is the most important element of your ad.

People flip through magazines and newspapers quickly. You have only a second or two to get them to stop and notice your ad. The headline plays a major role in stopping them, as does the visual.

The main purpose of the headline is to grab the reader's attention and make him or her notice and start reading your ad. You can achieve this in several ways. For example, here's an attention-grabbing headline from an ad published in a newspaper:

IMPORTANT NEWS FOR WOMEN WITH FLAT OR THINNING HAIR

This headline effectively gains the attention of the prospect for two reasons: it promises important news and it identifies the prospect for the service (women with flat or thinning hair). Incidentally, this ad persuaded more than 1,200 readers a month to clip a coupon and send for a free brochure on a hair-conditioning procedure.

To promote a home study course in writing for children, the Children's Institute of Literature has been using the same successful ad for decades. The headline reads:

WE'RE LOOKING FOR PEOPLE TO WRITE CHILDREN'S BOOKS

This headline works for several reasons. Like the "Thinning Hair" headline, it identifies the prospect for the service: people who want to write children's books. More important, it carefully delays any reference to the fact that the ad is selling a home study course, giving the reader sufficient time to get interested and involved before going into the offer. In fact, although the headline is completely honest, you get the impression initially that the ad is from a children's book publisher looking for authors ... which grabs the attention of the wanna-be authors who are prospects for this course.

A headline does not have to contain just one sentence or phrase set in one uniform type size. You can often create a more eye-catching and effective headline using what I call a three-part headline.

The first part, or kicker, is an "eyebrow" or short line that goes in the upper left-hand corner of the ad, either straight across or at a slant. One good use of the kicker is to select a specific type of reader for the ad (e.g., "Attention COBOL Programmers"). Another effective technique is to let the reader know you are offering something free (e.g., "Special Free Offer — See Coupon Below").

The second part, set in larger type, is your main headline, which states the central benefit or makes a powerful promise. The third part is your subhead, where you expand on the benefit or reveal the specific nature of the promise. Below are some examples of main headlines and subheads.

$500 A DAY WRITER'S UTOPIA

Here's the breakthrough offer that opens up a whole new world for writers or those who hope to become writers ...

FOR HIGH SPEED, HIGH PERFORMANCE DATA INTEGRATION, LOOK INTO MAGI MIRROR

Now you can move data instantly from one program to another, right from your PC screen.

If your headline is designed to arouse curiosity or grab attention but does so at the expense of clarity, be sure to make the nature of your proposition immediately clear in a subhead or within the first sentence. Otherwise you will lose the interest of the reader whose attention you worked so hard to gain.

3. Expand on the headline in the lead paragraph

The lead paragraph must rapidly follow up on the idea expressed in the headline. For instance, if the headline asks a question, the lead should immediately answer it. The promise made to the reader in the headline (e.g., "Learn the secret to richer, moister chocolate cake") must be fulfilled in the first few paragraphs of copy. Otherwise, the reader feels disappointed and turns the page. Here is an example from an ad selling a business opportunity:

QUIT YOUR JOB OR START PART TIME

Chimney Sweeps Are Urgently Needed Now

My name is Tom Risch. I'm going to show you how to make $200 a day saving people from dangerous chimney fires ...

Do not waste the reader's time with a "warm-up" paragraph. Instead, go straight to the heart of the matter. In editing a first draft, an important question to ask yourself is, "Can I eliminate my first paragraph and start with my second or third paragraph?" Eight times out of ten, you can — and the copy will be strengthened as a result.

After writing copy, read through the ad, taking note of the content of all headlines and subheads. Make certain the copy under each heading relates to the topic of the heading. Avoid subheads and heads that sound great but have nothing to do with

what's in the copy. Readers are good at spotting this, and it turns them off.

4. Use a layout that draws the reader into the ad

Using a layout that draws the reader into the ad is something that cannot be described in words but is experienced visually. Some ads will seem friendly, others inviting. And some will seem to draw your eye to the page and make reading a pleasure. This is the type of layout you want to use in your own ads. Avoid layouts that make the ad hard to read or discourage readers from even trying.

Your layout should have a focal point — a central, dominant visual element that draws the reader's eye to the page. This is usually the headline or the visual, but it might also be the coupon or perhaps the lead paragraph of copy. When there are two or more equally prominent visuals competing for the eye's attention, readers become confused and don't know where to start reading. Always make one element larger and more prominent than the others.

Ad body copy should be set in type no smaller than nine point, preferably ten point. Another way of putting this: the type size in the ad should be equal to or larger than the type size in the publication's articles.

Set the body copy in serif type. Serif type has curls and lines at the end of the letter stems, as in this book. It is easier to read than sans serif, which has no such markings at the end of the letter stems. Headlines can be set in either typeface.

Do not use reverse type (white on black). Avoid setting type against a colored background, illustration, or photograph. Use black type on a plain white background. It is easiest to read.

Buy several magazines. Go through them. Clip full-page ads that appeal to you visually or seem to stand out from the others and draw you in. Save these in a file. Emulate their layouts when designing your own ads.

5. Write body copy that supports and expands on the headline and opening

Which facts should be included in your body copy? Which should be left out? You can make this decision by listing all the key points and then deciding which are strongest and will best convince the reader to respond to your advertisement.

Start by listing all the features of your product and the benefits people get from each feature. For instance, a *feature* of an air conditioner is that it has a high energy efficiency rating; the *benefit* is a lower electric bill.

After making a complete list of features and benefits, list them in order of importance. Then begin your body copy with the most important benefit. Incorporate the rest of the benefits on your list until you have sufficient copy. This copy highlights the most important reasons to buy the product, given the space limitations of your ad.

Editing is an important part of writing good ads. You don't have the freedom to go on at length as you do in a brochure or direct mail package. But you do want to include all the important information. Here's one way to do it. First write the ad copy without regard to length. Get all your sales arguments in. Make the message complete. Then go back. Prune and edit. Trim the copy until it fits. This can be difficult. It's easy to fall in love with your copy and not want to cut any part of it. But you don't want to force the reader to use a magnifying glass to read your ad.

Chapter 10 gives additional guidelines for writing effective body copy.

6. Be specific

"Platitudes and generalities roll off the human understanding like water from a duck," writes Claude Hopkins in his classic book *Scientific Advertising*. "They leave no impression whatever."

The most common mistake I see in advertising today is "lazy copy" — copy written by copywriters who were too lazy to take the time to learn about their audience and understand the features and benefits of their product . . . the reasons why someone would want to buy it.

Why is so much ad copy vague and general? There are two reasons. First, it takes effort to research and understand information about products and markets. We avoid it because it's difficult, time-consuming work, and ads are usually written on tight deadlines. Either there isn't time to gather facts or, more frequently, the writer takes the easy route and writes only from the material immediately in front of him or her.

Second, some ad writers are not research oriented. Some do not believe specifics are important. Many feel tone and emotion are everything. They believe consumers do not want product facts. Experience shows that, for the most part, they are wrong.

Good advertising is effective largely because it is specific. There are two benefits to being specific: it gives the customer the information he or she needs before making a buying decision, and it creates believability. As Hopkins points out, people are more likely to believe a specific, factual claim than a boast, a superlative, or a generalization.

74

Does this mean ad copy should be a litany of facts and figures? No. But the copywriter's best weapon is the selective use of facts to support a sales pitch. Here are some examples of well-written, specific, factual copy, taken from real ads.

```
One out of every four
Americans has high blood
pressure. Yet only half
these people know it. You
may be one of them. If
you are over forty, you
owe it to yourself to
have your blood pressure
checked ...
```

```
The Mobilaire (R) 5000.
59 pounds of Westing-
house air conditioning
in a compact unit that
cools rooms 12' x 16' or
smaller. Carry one home,
install it in minutes —
it plugs in like a lamp
into any adequately
wired circuit. Fits any
window 19⅛" to 42" wide.
```

```
BluBlockers filter out
blue light making every-
thing appear sharper,
clearer and with a
greater 3-dimensional
look to it. Blue is the
shortest light wave in
the visible spectrum and
focuses slightly in
front of our retina which
is the focusing screen in
our eyes. By filtering
```

```
out the blue in the
BluBlocker lenses, our
vision is enhanced and
everything appears to
have a 3-dimensional
look to it. But there's
more ...
```

A report in *Direct Marketing* magazine describes an experiment in which more than 70 retailers tested different ads and measured results. Here's what they found: when advertisers doubled the number of product facts in the ad, sales increased approximately 50%.

7. Start with the prospect, not the product

Of course, your ad must contain information about the product. But the information must be *important to the readers* — information they will find interesting or fascinating, information that will answer their questions, satisfy their curiosity, or cause them to believe the claims you make. Information, in short, that will convince them to buy your product.

The reader's own concerns, needs, desires, fears, and problems are all more important to him or her than your product, your company, and your goals. Good advertising copy, as Jeffrey Lant points out, is "client-centered." It focuses on prospects and how your product solves their problems. Or as copywriter Don Hauptman puts it, "Start with the prospect, not your product."

For instance, instead of saying, "We have more than 50 service centers nationwide," translate this statement into a reader benefit: "You'll be assured of prompt, courteous service and fast delivery of replacement parts from one of our 50 service centers located nationwide." Don't say "energy efficient" when you can say "cuts your electric bills in half."

The real "star" of your ad is the reader. Your product is second and is only of concern in that it relates to a need, a desire, or a problem the reader has or a benefit he or she wants. Your company is a distant third — the least important element of your copy. It is only of concern if it reassures those prospects who want to do business with a well-known firm that has a good reputation and is financially stable. Here are excerpts from some ads that start with the prospects and their needs and concerns:

Whether you love computers or hate them, there's no avoiding it:

Today, computers are an essential tool for chemical engineers. To remain productive, you've got to keep up with the latest software and computing techniques.

But being a computer expert can be a full-time job.

The solution? You can go back to school and get a degree in computer science. Or, attend Chemputers '96.

Every day, law firms struggle with the expense and inconvenience of engraved and pre-printed stationery.

Now you can select the best mutual funds for any portfolio ... _faster and easier than ever ... to become a_ hero with your clients. And ensure that they invest their money with you, again and again.

Need extrusion wear parts that last longer? Ferro-Tic HT-6A is the answer.

Are you sick and tired of your current job?

Do you dream of a career that's fun, exciting — and financially rewarding?

Do you enjoy going on vacation, traveling to exotic locations, and seeing the world?

If so, the Echols International Tourism Institute has some exciting news for you about career opportunities in today's travel industry.

One way to increase readership and response is to promise the reader useful information in your headline and then deliver it in your ad copy. For an ad offering businesspeople a book on how to collect overdue bills, Milt Pierce wrote this headline:

The information-type ad is highly effective in mail order advertising. Why? Because so many mail order buyers are information seekers — much more so than the average consumer.

8. Write in a clear, simple, conversational, natural style

According to *Business Marketing* magazine's Copy Chasers, a panel of judges who regularly critique advertising in a monthly column, good ad copy should sound like "one friend talking to another."

I agree. Copy should not be pompous, remote, aloof, or written in "corporatese." The most effective copy is written in a plain, simple, conversational style — the way a sincere person talks when he or she wants to help or advise you.

Madison Avenue has created an accepted style for ad copy that the big agencies now use. This style seems to deliberately remind you that you are reading an ad. It is self-conscious copy. Avoid this type of slick lingo.

Read the sample copy scattered throughout this book. This is the type of natural-sounding tone you want to achieve. Also refer to chapter 10 for an in-depth discussion of how to write clear, concise body copy.

A deliberate attempt to achieve a certain style in copy usually has the effect of calling attention to the writing itself and diverting the reader away from the message.

It makes readers aware they are reading an ad. The focus should be on the prospect and the product, not on the ad or the copywriter. Even ads for technical products should sound friendly, inviting, and understandable. Here are some examples, taken from recent print ads, of copy that achieves the natural, easy-flowing tone you want in your ads.

The travel business is the world's fastest growing industry. Trained personnel are desperately needed by hotels ... airlines ... tour companies ... cruise lines ... convention centers ... and travel agencies — both here and abroad. Now Echols can give you the training to help you qualify.

Making dies, guides, die rings, die holders, mandrels, baskets, and fixtures from HT-6A enables your wear parts to work through millions of cycles. Dies last longer, reducing downtime and replacement costs in hot and cold extrusion processes.

You may have read that *today* the lending climate is friendlier. Don't believe it! The fact is, only *larger* corporations have ready access to capital. Growing businesses looking for funding are often up against a brick wall.

Chemputers is the only computer users conference specifically designed for chemical engineers. In just 48 hours, you'll learn things about computers ... and chemical engineering ... that your colleagues won't get in an entire year of reading journals and going to trade shows.

Your style may be slightly different. That's fine. But I have found that reader-friendly ads have several things in common: simple language, short sentences, and short paragraphs. Copy should address the reader directly; the word "you" should appear frequently.

Use informal language: contractions, sentence fragments. Use conversational language, even a slang phrase now and then, or colloquial expressions. A good ad sounds like one person talking to another about a subject of mutual interest.

9. Decide what you want readers to do next. Then ask them to do it — and make it easy

There are three steps for turning your ad into a response-generating marketing tool.

First, decide what type of response you want. What action do you want the reader to take? Do you want your prospect to phone or write you, or clip a coupon and mail it back to you? Do you want the reader to visit your store, request a copy of your catalogue or sales brochure, set up an appointment to see a salesperson, test-drive your product, or order your product directly from the ad?

Second, after you decide what you want the reader to do, tell the reader to do it. The last few paragraphs of your copy should spell out the action you want the reader to take and give him or her reasons to take it. For instance:

Just clip the coupon or call toll-free now and we'll send you this policy FREE without obligation as a special introduction to EMPLOY-MENT GUIDE.

So why not call 1-800-FINE4WD for a dealer convenient to you?

Just send in the card (or the coupon) and have some fun with your first issue. Then pay us *after* you've taken a look.

And send for DISPLAY MAS-TERS' invaluable FREE booklet on Point-of-Purchase Marketing, "33 Ways to Better Displays: What Every Marketing Executive Should Know

```
About Point-of-Purchase
Displays in Today's Mar-
ket."
```

Give the reader a reason to respond. These reasons can include —

- a free booklet or catalogue,
- a free brochure,
- a free bonus gift,
- a price list or cost estimate,
- a discount or sale,
- a time-limited offer,
- a free initial consultation or evaluation, or
- a no-obligation quotation.

The third step is to give the reader a mechanism for responding. Emphasize this mechanism in your ad layout to simplify the process of making contact with you.

In print advertising, this mechanism is usually a coupon included in the ad or a toll-free phone number, printed in large type to attract attention to itself. Some magazines allow you to insert a reply card, which is bound into the magazine and appears opposite your ad. This is an expensive technique, but it can dramatically increase replies.

Even if your ad is not primarily a response ad (and with rare exceptions, I can't understand why you wouldn't want response), you should still make it easy for your readers to get in touch with you should they want to do business with you. This means always including at least an address and telephone number and, in today's cyberspace universe, fax number, e-mail address, and Web site.

In a recent TV commercial, Long Island Lighting Company (Lilco) offered a free booklet on electricity. The ad informed viewers they could get the booklet by calling their local Lilco office — but no phone number was mentioned in the commercial. To respond, prospects were forced to check old utility bills or look up Lilco in the phone book.

This is a response-killing mentality that many advertisers embrace. I will never understand it. Why make it difficult for people to get in touch with you or order your product? It doesn't make sense.

e. SAMPLE AD

The best way to learn how to write full-page mail order space ads is to study successful ads. You know an ad is successful when you see it run again and again. If the ad were not profitable, the advertiser would not continue to run it. Sample #6 shows an ad you can study as a model of successful mail order ad copywriting.

All New Edition

How To Get Thousands of
FREE GIFTS

THE MOST INCREDIBLE COLLECTION OF FREE THINGS...EVER!

Imagine the thrill of walking to your mailbox every day and finding it overflowing with valuable gifts of every type and description.

No, it's not a dream. As a result of months of intensive research, we've uncovered thousands – yes, *THOUSANDS* – of fantastic free things. Every one is COMPLETELY FREE – nothing to buy, no gimmicks, no catches.

Here's a small sample of the free gifts waiting for *you* right now.

• **FREE** – Over 9,000 recipes – Why spend $8.00-$10.00 for just one cookbook when hundreds are yours – *ABSOLUTELY FREE?*

• **FREE** – Loads of products you use every day. Companies want you to try their products and will give you actual samples. Why pay for something that's FREE?

• **FREE – Gifts for the kids** • *FREE Baby Food* • **FREE Magazine Subscriptions** • *FREE Cassette tape* ($11.95 value) • **FREE Color Wall Posters** • *FREE Stamps & Coins*

• **FREE** TRAVEL GUIDES • *FREE BOOKS* – On hundreds of fascinating subjects • **FREE** CORRESPONDENCE COURSE • *FREE Gift from the President*

• **FREE From Uncle Sam** – The U.S. Government has over 400 *FREE* gifts, benefits & services just for the asking. Are you getting your share?

• **FREE** Guides – Learn How-To:
  ❏ Panel a room yourself
  ❏ Slash your gasoline costs
  ❏ Save hundreds heating your home
  ❏ Get out of debt forever
  ❏ Make...Save...Invest your money
  ❏ Protect your home
  ❏ Lose weight
  ❏ Buy more for less money
  ❏ Lots, LOTS more.

• **FREE Gifts just for Sports Fans** – your favorite team has all kinds of great free gifts waiting for you.

• **FREE From Social Security** – Don't miss out on any benefits. Social Security has a confidential report with your name on it that tells what benefits are coming to you.

• **FREE For You** – A carload of free things are waiting for you no matter what your interests – gardening, sewing, sports, careers, health, business, pets, cars, music, personal computers, hobbies, education, religion, bargain hunting – to mention just a few.

We put everything we discovered into a big 50,000 word book called *A Few Thousand of the Best FREE Things in America*. In it is everything you'll need – descriptions of each gift, over 200 illustrations, all necessary names and addresses and just what to ask for.

SPECIAL BONUS REPORT

• *"How to Get FREE Groceries & Gifts"* – Learn how one woman saves over $2,000 every year – an incredible 50% off her grocery bill – with *FREE GROCERIES!* This little-known (but perfectly legal) method is suprisingly easy to use when you know how.

10

DIRECT MAIL

Direct mail, once the standard vehicle for mail order sales, has become increasingly expensive. Before going this route in your mail order business, you will need to know how to evaluate whether you can make a profit using direct mail and how to create a direct mail package.

a. CAN YOU MAKE A PROFIT USING DIRECT MAIL?

1. Calculating the cost of direct mail

The cost of your mailing is critical. Your profit from a direct mailing is calculated by subtracting mailing costs from the net revenues generated (i.e., revenue after the cost of producing your direct mail package). The only ways to make direct mail more profitable are to increase the response rate or lower the cost of the direct mail package.

There are four items that are recurring costs that you incur every time you mail the package:

    (a) Mailing list rental

    (b) Printing of the components of the direct mail package

    (c) Production (i.e., the letter shop charge for assembling the mailings and preparing them for the post office)

    (d) Postage

The price of a direct mailing is usually measured in cost per thousand units mailed. Direct mail costs range from $400 to $750 per thousand, but can go higher. A more complex package with more elaborate components will cost more. You'll also pay more per unit to print and mail a small quantity of packages. On the other hand, you'll get volume discounts from the printer if you print and mail large quantities.

If you hire an ad agency, copywriter, or graphic design firm, the fees represent additional costs. These are considered start-up costs and are not factored into the cost per thousand calculation, which includes only the recurring costs — those costs you pay every time the piece is mailed.

2. Calculating your break-even point

Once you've figured out the cost of the mailing, you need to decide if you are likely to sell enough product through the mailing to break even or to make a profit.

Let's say you sell your product for $70, and your cost per unit to make and ship the product is $10. That means your net revenue on each sale is $70 minus $10, or $60.

If your cost per thousand in the mail is $600, you must generate a net revenue per thousand of $600 to break even on the mailing. This means you must get ten orders

81

per thousand pieces mailed — a 1% response rate.

Your direct mail package is going to cost you $400 to $700 per thousand in the mail regardless of the price of the product. Therefore, it is difficult to profitably sell inexpensive items through direct mail packages. If your product costs less than $30 to $40, you will have trouble making a profit using one-step direct mail. (For low-priced products, you are better off running small ads to generate leads and then using an inquiry fulfillment package to convert inquiries to sales, as outlined in chapters 7 and 8.)

Worksheet #3 is a form you can use to calculate mailing costs, net revenues, and break-even response rates. You may photocopy this form to use in your own business. Sample #7 shows the worksheet filled in for a fictitious mailing.

3. What response rate can you realistically hope to achieve?

For mail order direct mail packages, response rates can range from below 0.5% to 3% or higher. For many products, 1% to 2% is a typical response rate. If your calculations show you need a response much higher than 2% to break even, direct mail is not likely to be a successful way to sell your product.

b. WHERE DO YOU FIND GOOD LISTS?

Do you know what the most important part of your direct mail campaign is? It's not the copy. It's not the artwork. It's not even the format or when you mail. It is the mailing list.

A great mailing package with superior copy and scintillating design might pull double the response of a poorly conceived mailing. But the best list can pull a response ten times greater than the worst list for the identical mailing piece.

The most common direct mail mistake is not spending enough time and effort up front when you select — and then test — the list. Remember: in direct marketing, a mailing list is not just a way of reaching your market. It *is* the market.

The best list available to you is your "house" list — a list of customers and prospects who previously bought from you or responded to your ads, public relations campaigns, or other mailings. Typically, your house list will pull double the response of an outside list.

When renting outside lists, get your ad agency or list broker involved in the early stages. The mailing piece should not be written and designed until after the lists have been identified and selected.

For mail order offers, you want to rent response lists. These are lists from other mail order companies containing the names of customers who have bought by mail.

The more recently the buyers on the list placed their last order, the better. Some list owners rent "hotline names," which are lists of buyers who have bought very recently. If you can get hotline names, rent them. They usually outperform regular names.

Look for lists of mail order buyers whose average order is close to the sale price of your product. If you sell a $100 product, you may not do well with a list of people who buy $10 products.

People who buy more than once are considered better prospects than one-shot buyers. These multiple buyers, or "multi-buyers," can be rented separately on many mail order response lists.

WORKSHEET #3
DIRECT MARKETING ANALYSIS

Promotion_____Date_____

Gross margin per unit		Direct mail cost per unit	
Selling price		Circulars	
Add: Handling charge Total Revenue per unit		Letters	
Cost of merchandise		Inserts	
Shipping or delivery		Lift pieces	
Order processing		Envelopes	
Cost of returns		Order forms	
Bad debt		List rental	
Other		Assembly	
Total cost per unit		Addressing	
		Postage	
Gross margin per unit		Other	
		Direct mail cost per unit	

Net profit break-even point	
Units mailed	
Response rate	
Unit sales	
Gross margin	
Mailing costs	
Fixed costs	
Creative development	
Allocations other	
Total fixed costs	
Total net profit	
Break-even unit sales	
Break-even unit mailing	
Prepared by_____	

DIRECT MARKETING ANALYSIS

Promotion __MS TOOLKIT SOFTWARE__ Date __2/15/97__

Gross margin per unit		Direct mail cost per unit	
Selling price	$129	Circulars	$110
Add: Handling charge	$9	Letters	$120
Total Revenue per unit	$138		
Cost of merchandise	$6	Inserts	—
Shipping or delivery	$4	Lift pieces	—
Order processing	$2	Envelopes	$50
Cost of returns	—	Order forms	
Bad debt	—	List rental	$100
Other	—	Assembly	$15
Total cost per unit	$12	Addressing	$5
		Postage	$200
Gross margin per unit	$126	Other	—
		Direct mail cost per unit	$600

SAMPLE #7 — Continued

Net profit break-even point	
Units mailed	10,000
Response rate	2%
Unit sales	200
Gross margin	$25,200
Mailing costs	$6,000
Fixed costs	—
Creative development	—
Allocations other	—
Total fixed costs	$19,200
Total net profit	
Break-even unit sales	—
Break-even unit mailing	—
Prepared by R. Bly	

"Inquirers" are people who have made inquiries to a mail order company but who have not purchased. These prospects are not as good as buyers, and such lists should usually not be used.

Compiled lists are lists of likely customers within a given category (e.g., dog owners, mothers, chemical engineers, school teachers) that are compiled by a mailing list company for renting to mailers. These people may or may not have bought through the mail before, but you will have no idea whether they did or didn't. These lists are compiled from a variety of sources: new homeowners, telephone white or yellow pages, directories, tax files. One Florida company that offers a property-tax-reduction service sends lead-generating mailings to owners of property in one county, using a list of homeowners and commercial owners it obtains from that county. Compiled lists do not usually work for mail order offers.

c. PROVEN TECHNIQUES FOR WRITING A SUCCESSFUL DIRECT MAIL PACKAGE

Direct mail holds particular fascination for many marketers because it is one of the few promotional methods whose results can be measured directly and precisely (see chapter 14 for a discussion of testing). Here are 21 copywriting techniques that can make your direct mail package lively, fascinating, interesting, better read, and more effective at generating leads and sales.

1. Empathize with the reader

Direct mail professionals use the term "affinity group" to describe a market segment of people with similar interests. Stamp collectors, freelance writers, automobile enthusiasts, pet owners, IBM PC users, bodybuilders, and joggers are all examples of affinity groups.

Members of affinity groups often have strong feelings about, and interest in, their particular obsession. Perhaps you have "hacker" friends who talk endlessly about bits, bytes, boots, and other computer jargon. It may bore you silly. But to them, it's sheer joy. Do you have a special hobby or interest? If you do, you know how much fun it is to share it with other people.

When writing to affinity groups, empathize with their interests. Show that you are "in sync" with them, that you understand and support their particular cause. Here's an example of "empathy" copy from a letter offering a subscription to *Practical Homeowner*:

```
Dear Homeowner,

Do you enjoy your home?
I mean really enjoy it?
Does it still feel good
at the end of the day to
walk through that door,
kick off your shoes, and
just be . . . home?
```

By showing readers that you are sympathetic to their needs, you are already halfway to winning them over as friends . . . and as customers.

2. Use the "ah-ha" factor

One way to get readers on your side is to tell them something they already know.

The trick is not to tell them something mundane or something blatantly obvious but to bring to the surface a fact, feeling, or emotion they may not have openly acknowledged before. When they hear the fact or feeling stated openly by you, their reaction is "ah-ha" or "yes, of course" or "that's right!"

The power of this technique is that we all like to learn more about ourselves and our state of mind. The ah-ha technique builds your credibility with your prospect by reinforcing and dramatizing the reader's own knowledge or beliefs.

Here's an example from a letter selling a home study program on money management and investing:

```
Dear Reader:

My name is Morton Shul-
man. I am a medical doc-
tor by training, and I
still maintain an active
practice. I make a good
living as a doctor, but
I realized long ago that
you can't get rich on a
salary alone, not even a
doctor's salary. So I
turned to investing.
```

Most of us rely on our salaries, not investments, for income. We know deep down that we can't get rich this way, but because of laziness, lack of time, or lack of knowledge we don't do much about it. That's why Dr. Shulman's letter really hits home. When I read it, I said, "Yes, he's right; I ought to be smarter about handling my money." And that is the exact frame of mind a company selling an investment program would want to create.

3. Turn a potential negative into a positive

The following story is told by Jim Young in John Caples's classic book *Tested Advertising Methods*:

A few years ago there was a hail storm just before harvest. I had thousands of mail orders and checks, and almost every apple hail pocked. Problem: Should I send the checks back or risk dissatisfied customers? Actually these apples were damaged only in appearance. They were better eating than ever. Cold weather, when apples are ripening, improves their flavor. So I filled the orders. In every carton I put a printed card:

```
"Note the hail marks
which have caused minor
skin blemishes on some of
these apples. These are
proof of their growth at
a high mountain alti-
tude, where the sudden
chills from hail storms
help firm the flesh and
develop the natural
fruit sugars which give
these apples their in-
comparable flavor."
```

Not one customer complained. Next year I received orders which said: "Hail marked apples, if available; otherwise the ordinary kind."

This is a good example of how you can use words to alter the customer's perception of reality.

88

Another example of this technique is the advertisement in Harry and David's Fruit of the Month Club mail order catalogue for their famous Royal Riviera Pears. For years the copy has said of these pears: "So unusual that not one person in a thousand has ever tasted them." Makes you yearn for a bite so much that you never stop to think that this fancy phrase also says, "Not too many people buy this product." Another instance of copy turning a negative into a positive.

4. Ask a provocative question

"Do you want me to give you a surefire way of improving direct mail response?" That's an example of using a question to grab the reader's attention and heighten interest.

Question leads can be extremely effective if the lead —

(a) arouses the reader's curiosity,

(b) deals with a timely, important, or controversial issue, or

(c) asks a question to which the reader genuinely wants the answer.

Some examples:

```
WHAT DO JAPANESE
MANAGERS HAVE THAT
AMERICAN MANAGERS
SOMETIMES LACK?
(THE ECONOMICS PRESS)
```

```
IF YOU WERE TO FIND OUT
TODAY THAT YOU HAD ONLY A
SHORT TIME TO LIVE, WOULD
YOU FEEL COMFORTABLE WITH
THE AMOUNT OF LIFE INSUR-
ANCE THAT YOU HAVE PRO-
VIDED YOUR FAMILY?
(UNITED OF OMAHA)
```

```
IS THERE A ROLL OF FILM
IN YOUR CAMERA RIGHT NOW?
(KODAK)
```

5. Make a quick transition from your attention-grabbing opening to the sales pitch

Don't waste time with warm-up paragraphs. After grabbing the reader's attention, quickly shift the focus and begin making your sales pitch. People are busy and appreciate letters that get right to the point. In a brilliant fund-raising letter, the American Red Cross makes a fast transition from the reader's concerns to the Red Cross's plight in only two sentences:

```
Dear Friend:
When disaster strikes
your home you may ur-
gently need the Red
Cross.
But right now during the
holiday season the Red
Cross urgently needs you
. . .
```

6. Use details

Be specific. Do not be content to merely claim that a product is better, faster, easier, or cheaper when you can say how much better, how much faster, how much easier, or how much less it costs. Give the specific figures and facts. It makes copy interesting and believable. As copywriter Don Hauptman puts it: "Superlatives are often not credible; concretes invariably have the ring of truth."

In a promotional mailing piece, Click, a New Jersey–based messenger service, makes the specific claim, "We will pick up and deliver to Manhattan, on the same day, for only $9.50." This motivated me to try their service, and I have been a customer ever since.

I received another mailing, this one from a company asking if I wanted to earn part-time income selling its product. The visual showed a picture of the owner holding up a check; the caption read: "I'll send you a check for $4,154.65 for selling just one order." Using a specific number somehow makes the proposition seem more real and believable than a rounded-off figure or range of figures.

7. Be sincere

When asked by *Direct Marketing* magazine to name the most important characteristics of a copywriter, direct mail expert Ed McClean included "honesty" in his answer. And in a recent survey, when the Simmons Market Research Bureau asked people what they disliked most about direct marketing, 41% cited deception as their answer.

Contrary to the image the general public might have of direct marketing, the majority of direct marketing professionals are honest and strive to tell the truth in their mailings.

This isn't entirely altruistic, of course. Through experience, we have learned that while we might be able to trick the customer with deceptive advertising once, a buyer who feels duped will not buy from us a second time. And repeat sales represent the bulk of profits in most business enterprises. So it is more profitable to be honest than to be deceptive or misleading or to tell outright lies.

People are turned off by direct mail that seems insincere, too high-pressure, or dishonest. But how can you sound sincere in your letters?

To start, *be* sincere. Tell the truth. If you don't believe what you are saying, it will come through in the copy.

Second, ask other people to read your letters and see if your copy has the "ring of truth." Even an honest salesperson, in his or her zeal to sell the product, may overstate the case and sound like a phony.

Woodbridge Memorial Gardens sent my wife and me a letter that failed to convince us of their concern for our well-being. It begins:

```
Dear Neighbor:
It is very disturbing to
me to think that you may
lose the last opportunity
to   own   your   personal,
aboveground mausoleum at
a price that can save you
so much money and heart-
ache.
```

Maybe we're cynics. But we would have found the letter more credible if the writer said "I am concerned." "Disturbed" seemed to be overstating the case.

Another letter that failed to motivate us was this fund-raising solicitation from the American Kidney Fund.

```
Dear Friend:
I wouldn't write you like
this if it weren't truly
urgent.
```

Our reaction? "Of course you would. It's your job to raise funds. What else would you be doing with your time aside from writing to people like us?"

8. Avoid contradictions

When reviewing your copy, be sure to check for consistency and eliminate contradictions between statements. If you are not consistent with facts and statements, you are automatically wrong at least part of the time.

When people read contradictory statements in a letter or brochure, it destroys your credibility. Their reaction is: "These people don't know what they're talking about!"

A factual error is much worse than any grammatical error or typo you can make.

For example, Condé Nast recently ran an ad in *Advertising Age,* the purpose of which was to convince companies to run their ads in *Vogue, Glamour,* and other Condé Nast women's magazines. The copywriter used Debbi Fields, a successful entrepreneur, as an example of the kind of women who read these publications:

```
Debbi Fields is the cut-
above kind of woman ad-
vertisers dream about.
There are 26 million
women readers a lot like
her in the Condé Nast
Women's Package.
```

See the contradiction? How can a woman be a cut above the rest and yet be just like 26 million other women (approximately one quarter of the entire adult female population of the United States)? Believability is severely damaged.

9. Narrow the focus

The narrower your audience, the more specific you can be about meeting their needs. When people see their specific requirements addressed in an ad or mailer, they are more likely to respond than if the ad is making a broad appeal to all readers.

Let's say you give seminars in business strategy. One possible headline for your seminar mailing is:

BUSINESS STRATEGY

What's unique about your business strategy seminar that could separate it from dozens of other similar seminars being offered? Perhaps you emphasize doing business on an international scale. You could change the title to read:

GLOBAL BUSINESS STRATEGY

Better. Now, if you tailor your seminar to different industries, you can focus the headline even tighter by targeting those industries. For example:

GLOBAL BUSINESS STRATEGY IN THE CHEMICAL INDUSTRY

Chemical Week takes this one step further with a seminar called:

GLOBAL BUSINESS STRATEGY IN THE LUBRICANT ADDITIVES INDUSTRY

See the improvement? If the lubricant additives industry is a big enough market to warrant a separate promotional effort, then *Chemical Week,* offering a seminar geared toward the industry's specific business needs will probably do much better than a company that offers general business seminars.

10. Make your product sound irresistible

The master of this technique is the person who writes the mailings and catalogue copy for Oregon-based Harry and David's Fruit of the Month Club. Want to get your mouth watering? Listen to how they describe their pound cake:

```
Few things are finer on
a summer's eve than a
slice of this buttery
loaf cake, heaped with
fresh, naturally sweet
Oregold slices. Top with
whipped cream, or a lit-
tle raspberry syrup,
makes a deliciously dif-
ferent gift ...
```

Here's how they describe peaches:

```
Huge, luscious peaches
grown right here in the
Rogue River Valley,
where rich volcanic
soil, crisp cool nights
and pure mountain water
nurture these beauties
to juicy, plump perfec-
tion. Shipped so fresh
you can almost smell the
orchards in bloom!
```

11. Use fear as a motivator

There are only two reasons why people do things: to gain rewards and to avoid punishment. Of the two, avoidance of punishment is often more powerful than the promise of gains.

Many advertisers avoid using fear as a motivator because they think it is a "negative" sell and they prefer to promote positives. This can be a costly error. Fear is one of the most powerful of human motivators. Fear sells us on many things, including alarm systems, life insurance, home medical tests, and childproof medicine bottles. Use it to your advantage when appropriate.

A recent mailing from American Family Publishers included a letter from (who else?) Ed McMahon. While the central theme of the promotion was "Enter the contest and win $10 million," Ed's lift letter approached it from a different angle. Namely, if you don't enter, you could be losing $10 million.

"If you return the winning number in time, I'll be personally handing you the first ten million dollars," says the letter.

"But, if you decide to ignore this letter and throw your exclusive numbers away, I'll surely be awarding all the money to someone else.

"PREVIOUS WINNERS HAVE THROWN THEIR NUMBERS RIGHT INTO THE TRASH — THEY LITERALLY THREW AWAY MILLIONS!"

This approach is tremendously effective. We all have a little nagging voice that tells us whenever we throw away a sweepstakes mailing, we could be throwing away a chance at a million dollars. But because we're busy, we go ahead and trash it anyway. This letter plays on that fear. It stops the busy person from throwing away the mailing and persuades him or her to enter the drawing.

12. Address the prospect's most common complaint

If you can anticipate your prospect's biggest complaint, objection, or problem with your product or service, answer it right at the start of your letter and you'll hook the reader into your sales pitch, creating a lot of goodwill in the process.

For instance, I feel that the public TV station in my area is a little hypocritical. After all, what's the point of eliminating commercial interruption if there's a fund-raising drive on the air every 20 minutes?

I recently received a fund-raising letter from the station. And guess what it says in its letter?

```
For years, people like
you have commented ...
"I'll tell you why I
don't give to THIRTEEN.
It's those pledge
drives! If you would just
take those drives off the
air and give me the in-
telligent TV I love, then
I'd become a member!"

Well, last year we took
you up on this challenge
by canceling two of our
three life sustaining
pledge drives. And,
we're going to take this
huge gamble again.
```

The message here is: "Hey, we listened to your complaints and we did what you asked. Now how about helping us out in return?"

13. Make your offer in the first few paragraphs

If you suspect that people are not likely to read your letter, you can boost the response by making your offer right up front. This way, the reader who only glances at the opening of your letter still gets the gist of the sales letter and learns about your offer.

Here's the opening of a letter promoting life insurance policies for children. A free booklet containing details of the insurance is offered right up front.

```
There's no gift more
meaningful ... for the
children you love than
the one discussed in a
new free pamphlet. It is
yours with my compli-
ments if you'll just mail
the card enclosed.
```

And this is the opening paragraph from a mailing offering a free brochure on a new 3M system for creating color slides and overheads:

```
Our free brochure tells
how you can make sophis-
ticated slides and over-
head transparencies . . .
over the phone, in min-
utes!
```

14. Flatter the reader

As long as you don't overdo it, flattery will get you everywhere. Or almost everywhere. The American Museum of Natural History mailed a letter that portrayed us, the recipients, as more noble and good than we really are:

Dear Reader:

From all indications available to us, you're a rather uncommon person. One who has a special reverence for our natural surroundings ... an endless and respectful curiosity about the quirks of animal and human nature ... an unabashed sense of wonder and fascination in the presence of our legacy from the past.

15. Inject the writer's personality and background into the copy

Make your copy personal. In some situations, especially those where the product or offer involves the prospect on a personal level, a human touch can add drama and impact to your mailing piece. For example, if you are offering seminars on public speaking, and you had a humiliating childhood experience while giving a presentation to your third-grade classmates, it can form the basis of a very personal letter in which you empathize with similar experiences the prospect may have had. Here's the opening of a hard-hitting, personal fund-raising appeal:

Dear Ms. Smith:

Do you remember me? I am Don McNeill and I was privileged to come into the homes of millions of Americans like you during the more than 30 years that I hosted "The Breakfast Club" on ABC radio.

I am now involved in one of the most important battles of my life — the battle to find a cure for Alzheimer's Disease.

This cruel disease killed my late wife, Kay. My concern now is for the 120,000 people who will die of Alzheimer's Disease this year, next year, and each year thereafter ...

Obviously, the personal nature of this note strikes a chord. Readers cannot help but feel sympathy for the writer and for his cause.

16. Highlight your guarantee

A strong guarantee is a great reassurance to people who haven't done business with you before. Companies that bury their guarantees in fine print instead of shouting about them up front are making an error.

A self-mailer (a flyer that can be sent without an envelope) from Atlantic Fasteners shows a picture of company president Patrick J. O'Toole holding up a certificate good for a $50 credit on the purchase of any fasteners sold by his firm. The headline and subhead underneath the photo read:

YOU GET NEXT-DAY DELIVERY FROM OUR STOCK OF 28,981,000 FASTENERS, OR I SEND YOU A $50 CREDIT! Only two credits issued in last 9,322 orders.

Give your guarantee a greater emphasis than it is now receiving. See what happens.

At worst, people will come to think of you as trustworthy. More likely, you'll get more orders out of the deal.

Are you worried that by stressing your guarantee, you'll get more people taking advantage of it? Stop worrying. The experience of hundreds of mail order companies indicates that people are basically honest. Only an insignificant percentage of people will try to dupe you.

Make your guarantee generous, long-term, and unconditional. A 30-day money-back guarantee will usually pull more orders than a 10-day money-back guarantee. A 60- or 90-day guarantee is even better.

17. Make it easy to respond

The easier you make it to reply to your mailing, the more replies you'll get.

How do you simplify the response process?

(a) Provide both a write-in and telephone option. Some people prefer to write and others prefer to call.

(b) Include your fax number and e-mail address.

(c) Use a loose reply card or order form rather than a reply element that has to be separated from a letter or brochure.

(d) Don't ask a lot of questions. Just get the minimum amount of information you need to fulfill the reader's order or request.

(e) Leave plenty of room for the reader to write in the required information on the reply form.

(f) Better yet, fill in the reply form for the reader, either with computer printing or by affixing a label.

(g) Pay the postage. Do not ask the reader to supply a stamp.

(h) When seeking orders, provide a toll-free number and accept major credit cards. According to InfoMat Marketing, a California-based ad agency specializing in direct response, credit card purchases and a toll-free number can increase your response by as much as 30%.

(i) When seeking inquiries or orders from business customers, include your fax number and encourage the recipient to fax the completed order form to you. Make sure the reply form is on white paper or other light-colored stock to ensure readability when it is faxed.

18. Use the two most powerful words in direct mail copywriting: "free" and "you"

Your copy should address the reader directly, as a person. As I said earlier, readers are not concerned with your company, your product, or whether you turn a profit. They are only concerned with their own problems, happiness, security, wealth. That's why your copy should talk about your reader, not yourself.

You can achieve this through a liberal use of the word "you" in your copy. When you review your copy, make sure you are using "you" frequently. A lot of "you's" indicate that you are speaking directly to the reader.

If you see a lot of "I, I, I" or "we, we, we" or "our company," you know your copy is off base. It is too we-oriented when it should be you-oriented. Fix it.

Here's a piece of copy that does a good job of speaking directly to the reader

YOU ASKED FOR THE FULL STORY OF THE SANDIER SELLING SYSTEM . . .

. . . and here it is. But the real story is about you — about how you can take a giant step up, right now. A step up — in the number of sales you close . . . the quality of those sales . . . the money you make. And just as important, an enormous gain in satisfaction and professional pride.

Don't forget the other magic word of direct mail copywriting: "Free."

People love to get free things. If you are generating leads and offering a brochure or catalogue, say that it is free. If you are selling a product and offering a premium, stress the free gift. If you offer a money-back guarantee, say the customer can examine your product on a risk-free trial basis.

On the outer envelope for one of his many successful mail order promotions, copywriter Andrew Linick uses the following teaser copy to highlight his free offer:

Act within 15 days to receive your FREE Gift worth $10!!!

Even a simple teaser such as "Special FREE offer inside" can get people who would otherwise not be tempted by your offer to open the envelope.

19. Give the reader useful or important information

Many people today are drowning in paper: direct mail, business correspondence, magazines, books, newspapers, reports.

Even so, if you can give your readers important information — something that can really improve their lives, protect their families, help them do their jobs better, or increase their incomes — they will be inclined to pay attention to you.

Direct mail has a big advantage over ads and articles. An ad or article competes with all the other ads and articles in the magazine, so it's likely to go unread. But a self-mailer or envelope is separate from all the other mailers and envelopes in your mailbox. Most readers will at least glance at it before making a "read/no read" decision.

One official-looking envelope that caught my attention was from the American Institute for Cancer Research. In big, bold type, the teaser shouted:

UPDATED SURVEY ON DIET AND CANCER

IMPORTANT: The Enclosed Survey is reserved in your name. You are requested to complete and return your survey.

Since most of us are concerned about diet and cancer, this kind of pitch will get our attention. Any information we receive that will help us eat healthier and live longer is welcome. Inside the envelope, unfortunately, was no information but a blatant fund-raising pitch. Had the organization enclosed a helpful booklet or article reprint, I might have been more inclined to contribute.

96

20. Demonstrate your product

If there is any way you can economically demonstrate your product in your mailing, do it. Few things are as convincing as an actual demonstration.

One of my favorite industrial promotions of all time advertised a chemical used in fireproofing. The headline of the ad commanded the reader to "TRY BURNING THIS COUPON." A match would set the page ablaze. But when you removed the match, the fire went out. Upon reading the copy, you learned that the page (produced by the manufacturer and bound as an insert into the magazine) was treated with the fireproofing compound being advertised. A brilliant example of a demonstration in print.

How do you demonstrate your product in direct mail? Remember, a mailing doesn't have to be just a brochure and a letter. You can include a product sample, a demo diskette, a test kit, a material swatch. There are many opportunities to let the customer try your product before ordering.

Seton Name Plate sent me a sample property identification plate along with a letter of instruction that began:

```
Try this simple test.
With a ball-point pen,
write your initials next
to the numbers on the
enclosed sample plate.
Now try to erase both.
Let me save you the
trouble . . . you can't
erase them without de-
facing the tag.
```

Customers don't have to take Seton's word that the plates are permanent. They can see it for themselves. Believability is increased perhaps a hundredfold.

21. Promise to share a secret

Exclusivity is another powerful direct mail motivator. People like to feel that they are getting inside information, becoming the first on their block to get a new possession, or getting in on the ground floor of a good deal.

Boardroom Classics, a book publisher, uses a six-page letter to sell its $29.95 *Book of Inside Information*. The headline of the letter reads:

```
WHAT CREDIT CARD COMPA-
NIES DON'T TELL YOU. PAGE
10.

What hospitals don't
tell you. Page 421.

What the IRS doesn't tell
you. Page 115.

What the airlines don't
tell you. Page 367.

What car dealers don't
tell you . . . (etc.)
```

I know this letter is successful because Boardroom mailed it to me five times or more within a 12-month period. The company would not repeat it so frequently if it were unprofitable. And Boardroom enjoys a reputation as one of the most successful direct marketers of books, newsletters, and other information products.

Overall, repeat mailings are a good indicator of what is working for other advertisers in direct mail. If a mailing is not generating good results, most mailers will mail it only once. Therefore, a repeat mailing usually indicates a healthy response.

d. SAMPLE DIRECT MAIL LETTER

Sample #8 shows an example of a letter from the newsletter *Practical Gourmet* offering information on fine food and wine.

BUY TWO, GET ONE FREE, AND BECOME

THE ENVY OF FRIENDS AND ASSOCIATES!

Dear Cooking Enthusiast:

Here's how you can turn out gourmet meals even on a limited budget. Same time in the kitchen. Receive compliments galore. SAVE MONEY TOO!

We are the publisher of The Practical Gourmet, a newsletter on gourmet cooking for everyone who enjoys good food, good wine, and lots of admiration.

In addition, we have developed for those who appreciate good food six timely Exclusive Reports and a Wine-Buying Guide that fits in your wallet.

(It can make you almost an instant connoisseur.)

1. The Pactical Guide to Cupboard, Refrigerator, and Freezer Storage. Ever have food spoil or "burn"? You know how costly that can be — and dangerous to your health. But never again when you follow the life-saving, money-saving tips in this handy guide.

2. Time Saving Tricks in Your Kitchen. No extra steps for you. No sticking to centuries-old techniques when a modern shortcut will do the job. Here's proof you too can prepare gourmet meals quickly.

3. New Ways with Fruit. Fresh, canned, and frozen fruit can bring gourmet surprises most cooks never know about.

4. Secrets of Cooking for Two. No longer will it be too much trouble to whip up a delightful meal just for you and your loved one. And you'll never again waste food, have too many leftovers, or complain about sameness.

5. Money-Saving Tips for Home Appliances. You know what a fortune it costs today to run or repair your refrigerator, dishwasher, dryer. Here's how they can save you money in unexpected ways.

6. Seafood Heritage from the Plains to the Pacific. Now making delicious seafood is a snap with this treasury of the secrets of master chefs — mouthwatering ideas and recipes you probably never heard of before.

7. Your Private Wallet-size Wine Buying Guide. Tells you at a glance which "specials" are true bargains, which are inferior vintages, which wines are the best from around the world.

Yes, the exclusive Special Reports and Wine Card described can make almost anybody a better cook . . . save time and money . . . win compliments galore.

They were created primarily for our subscribers, but we printed additional copies which we are now making available to cooking enthusiasts while the supply lasts.

And at BIG SAVINGS TOO!

Each Report sells for $3; the Wine Buying Guide for $2.

But you may buy any two Reports and receive a third one FREE; or buy four Reports, receive the other two, plus the Wine Guide, FREE. That's a $20 Value for only $12.

However, our supply is limited and this offer may not be repeated again. If you'd like to take advantage of it, please fill out and return the enclosed Money-Saving Certificate today!

Sincerely yours,

Andrew S. Linick
President

P.S. The Wine Buying Guide covers Red Burgundy, Red Bordeaux, White Bordeaux, White Burgundy, and Champagne from France; California Wine and German Wine from 1960. All on a handy card that fits in your wallet. Only $2 — or FREE with a complete set of Special Reports at the low money-saving rate. So send for yours today, while there are still cards available.

11
MAIL ORDER ON THE INTERNET

Marketing in cyberspace is a hot topic. Unless you live in a cave or on a deserted island, you will have heard about the Internet and how it is revolutionizing the way computer users communicate — and how businesses market their products and services.

But can you generate inquiries and orders on-line? Yes! The Internet offers you an opportunity to use low-cost, on-line media to produce additional revenues for your mail order operation.

The growth of the Internet has also created a new medium for advertisers and their copywriters: Web pages. (I give you some tips for creating an effective Web site and writing copy for Web pages later in the chapter.)

a. A BRIEF INTRODUCTION TO THE WEB

To keep things simple, let's start with a few definitions. The *Internet* is a large network by which virtually every computer in the world can be connected to virtually every other computer in the world.

The *World Wide Web* is a subsegment of the Internet. The Web consists of about a million computers, known as servers, that store information designed to be accessible to people who surf the Web. *Surfing,* also known as navigating or browsing, is what you do when you look through the files on these computers and find information of particular interest to you.

The information is divided into segments, each accessible using a different code. These segments are called *Web sites.* A server containing the text and graphics of one or more Web sites is said to be *hosting* those sites.

The first page of the Web site is the *home page.* This is usually the first thing a Web surfer sees when accessing any given Web site. Think of the home page as a table of contents and brief introduction combined into a single concise page.

Just as the table of contents in a book leads the reader to other pages, the home page leads the Web browser to other pages, known as *Web pages.* The two main elements of any Web site are the home page and Web pages.

A third element is the *hypertext links.* These are electronic links that help browsers immediately find information of interest to them within or between Web sites.

To show how these links work, let's compare Web pages to the printed page. In his bestselling book *Dianetics,* L. Ron Hubbard used a printed version of the hypertext concept. Hubbard believed the only reason people could not understand text was because they didn't know the meanings of one or more of the words. Therefore, in *Dianetics,* each new word or concept is highlighted in **bold**. This signals the reader to look for the definition at the bottom of the page. The highlight is the link that refers the reader to another section of the text.

Hypertext links on the Web work similarly. Any time there is a word the Web browser might want more detailed information on, that word is highlighted by putting it in a different color on the screen and underlining it.

To find out more, the Web browser clicks on the word with his or her mouse. The computer immediately displays a Web page that gives more detailed information on that particular subject.

This explanation is no substitute for actually getting on the Web and surfing it yourself. If you are going to write Web pages, you must become familiar with the World Wide Web. The only way to do this is to get on the Web and browse.

b. GETTING ON-LINE

Getting on-line isn't difficult. You need a computer, a modem, a telephone line, an Internet Service Provider (ISP), and browser software such as Netscape or Microsoft Internet Explorer. You can find an ISP by checking ads in the business section of your local paper, looking in the Yellow Pages, or asking your local computer store or consultant. Most ISPs provide the browser free when you sign on for their service. You can also access the Internet through the major on-line services including America On-Line and CompuServe.

As this book goes to press, more than 60 million people worldwide use the Internet and more than 17 million Americans browse the World Wide Web at least once a week. There are more than seven million home pages on the World Wide Web. Jeffrey Lant, an Internet marketing consultant, says this number is expected to increase to an incredible one billion home pages within a few years.

To target your Web copy to this special audience, consider its demographics:

- 75% of the Web audience are between the ages of 16 and 44.
- 55% of Web surfers have incomes over $55,000 a year.
- 54% have college degrees, and 26% have graduate degrees.
- 7 out of 10 business users surf the Web for production information and evaluation.
- Web surfing by business prospects is projected to double over the next 18 months.

c. WRITING EFFECTIVE COPY FOR THE WEB

1. Determine your objective before you begin to write

Marlene Brown, an authority on Internet marketing and author of the book *Techno Trends,* says the first step in creating a Web site is to determine what your objectives are. Do you want to sell products? Promote your programs and services? Build traffic on your home page? Clearly set out your objectives, then establish what measurable goals will indicate success.

Define your target audience. Who are your best prospects? Where are they? Do you want to advertise your products generically, or target your audience? Browse through computer bulletin boards, join discussion groups, and share ideas on e-mail lists to find out what is in demand and who wants to buy it.

"Surveys are a great way to get information about what Internet people think of your products, especially new ones you may launch or a series of related products you plan to bundle," says Brown. "Surveys prevent us from wasting time on products for which there is not a big market and give us ideas on needs."

The Web is, in a sense, a low-cost, electronic version of traditional direct marketing. Like traditional direct marketing, Internet marketing can generate an immediate, tangible, measurable response. But you can't know whether you are getting a good or bad result unless you establish objectives and then measure your results against these objectives.

After your Web site is operational for a few months, you'll have a better idea of what you can realistically expect to achieve and can adjust your objectives accordingly. At the same time, read articles in the business press to find out the results others are getting with their Web sites. This gives you a goal to shoot for.

2. Register a domain name people will look for

The domain name is the key part of the code the Web surfer types to reach your Web site. To reach my Web site, for example, type *http://www.bly.com*. The domain name is *bly.com*.

Your ISP, or whatever firm you select to host your Web site, can register a domain name for you. Choose a domain name that

people are likely to guess as yours. Reason: although there are many easy-to-use *search engines* (a search engine is a tool you can use to search the Web for home pages of interest to you according to subject matter and source), many new Web browsers don't know how to use them or don't bother to use them. Therefore, they are more likely to type in a few guesses until they hit on your domain name and can access your Web site. For instance, the domain name for the BOC Group, a large industrial manufacturer, is — logically — *BOC.com*. The domain name for Bob Bly is *bly.com*. I could also have chosen *BOB-BLY.com*.

You should choose a domain name that is either identical to or close to your company name, or one that relates to the category of product or service you provide. For instance, if you are a large freight forwarder, you might select *freight.com* or *ship.com*. If your company name is Global Transportation, you might chose *global.com* or *globtrans.com*.

Domain names are unique. If your competitor registers a domain name, no one else can use it. However, you can always register a variation of the name if that variation is still available. For example, if *barbecue.com* is taken, perhaps you will want to register *BBQ.com*, *barbecu.com*, or maybe *grill.com* — all good choices for a manufacturer of barbecue grills.

3. Use a "Web site under construction" sign

After you have arranged server space for your Web site with an ISP or other Web company and had the ISP register a domain name for you, your Web site will be "live." This means that people who type your domain name into their Web browsers will be sent to the site. Unfortunately, the site will be blank — empty — because you haven't put anything on it.

How long does it take to build a Web site? A small one- or two-person business can put up a simple Web site with a home page and a few Web pages in a couple of weeks or sooner. If you have a medium-size company, figure four to ten weeks to create your Web site. And I've seen large corporations, with multiple companies and divisions, take 6 to 12 months to develop their Web sites. The Web sites of big corporations can be so involved that a new job title, *Web Master*, has been created within the corporate world. The Web Master is the manager in charge of the corporate Web.

Since the day you have content on your Web site may well be several weeks or months after your site becomes operational, you don't want people to seek out your site and find it empty. Here's what to do. Put up some boilerplate copy about your company and its products and services on the home page. Include contact information — phone number, fax number, e-mail — so people interested in learning more can contact you directly, even though your Web site does not yet have a mechanism for direct response through the Web (it will — see section **8.** below). You can write something specifically for the Web site or scan, edit, and put on the site existing boilerplate copy from a corporate capabilities brochure, backgrounder press release, or other existing marketing documents.

This non-interactive message puts your message on the World Wide Web until your full Web site is ready, so visits to your site are not wasted. Above this descriptive copy, put a box with text that says, in large bold letters, "WEB SITE UNDER CONSTRUCTION." This tells visitors to your site that this is a temporary, not a permanent, site, so they shouldn't be put off by the lack of functionality, design, and detailed content . . . all of which are to come.

Interestingly, many ISPs automatically provide 8 megabytes (MB) of server space for your Web site at no extra charge when you use them to provide your Internet access. My guess is that there are thousands of ISP customers who have, in effect, paid for server space on which they could put a Web site and don't even know it. As of this writing, even CompuServe customers automatically get 1 MB of server space at no charge. Yet how many CompuServe users do you think have this space and don't use it?

4. Make your copy modular

The Web is a truly modular medium. The information you put up on your Web site must be divided into separate pages. These pages are electronically connected, but the Web browser need not go through them sequentially. He or she can skip back and forth from page to page, looking for information of interest.

Write and design your Web site with this in mind. Break your text into modules, the way you would break a training course into segments or a manual into chapters.

Make the text within each Web page modular as well. Don't make the page a solid block of text, as in a book. Break it up into four or five sections, each with its own subhead. This is the way Web browsers prefer to digest information — in short, bite-size chunks.

5. Keep it short and simple

Web pages are, in many ways, strikingly similar to regular printed prose. They are written in plain, simple, everyday English; no special language, computer codes, diagrams, or flow charts are used in place of conventional sentences and paragraphs.

The beauty of the World Wide Web is that information can be presented and accessed in layers. This is what enables you to keep your Web pages brief while still offering more detailed information to those who are interested.

If there is a difference, aside from hypertext links, between the printed page and on-line writing, it's that Web-page copy must be brief. There is no need to make Web pages longer than a page or two, since if there is more detailed information, the Web surfer can be directed to a separate on-line document with that information (using a hypertext link).

Most of your Web pages should be one to one-and-a-half pages long. If the page looks as though it will exceed two pages, break it into two separate subject pages and connect them with a hypertext link.

Keep paragraphs on Web pages short. Most paragraphs should be no longer than three to four lines. An occasional longer paragraph is okay, but when in doubt, break long paragraphs into two or more shorter paragraphs.

6. Use internal hypertext links as an on-line index

In a printed book, you turn to the index in the back, look up a subject by name, then turn to the pages where this information is located. With on-line writing, the document itself is its own index. Key words are highlighted and linked to other sections of the document.

Do not overdo the links. If every other word is underlined, highlighted, and hyperlinked, it will confuse readers and they won't click on anything. Highlight only those key topics that you want the prospect to explore further. If you break up a Web page into sections with subtopics separated by subheadings, you shouldn't have more than one hypertext link per section or more than four or five per Web page.

7. Use external hypertext links to increase visits to your Web site

One type of hypertext link connects Web pages within a Web site. You can also put in links that instantly transport your prospect to the home pages of other advertisers or organizations.

For example, if you sell pet supplies, it would be natural to link your Web site to the home page of the American Cat Breeders' Association. If you sell desktop publishing software, a link to a Macintosh user's group such as MacSciTech makes sense, as would a link to the Apple Computer Web site. You get the idea.

In return, you want these advertisers or organizations to hyperlink their sites to your home page, so that browsers visiting the American Cat Breeders' Association or the Apple Computer Web sites are able to hit a link that will bring them to your home page. By arranging these strategic hypertext links, you can increase visits to your own site (by bringing browsers from these other sites to your own home page), as well as improve the usefulness of your site (by helping browsers access related relevant information on other home pages).

Another good way to increase visits (or "hits") to your Web site is to have hyperlinks between your site and the sites of other mail order entrepreneurs selling related products. Some may be willing to give you a free link from their site if you give them a free link from your site in return. Others may want to charge you a fee.

8. Give people a reason to complete your enrollment page

Every business Web site should have an enrollment page. The *enrollment page* is a Web page where visitors to your site can register, giving you key information including their name, company, title, address, phone and fax numbers, and e-mail address.

For the Web advertiser, the enrollment page is an extremely valuable tool. It allows you to more accurately measure Web response, provides a vehicle prospects can use to request additional information, and enables you to build a prospecting data base that includes, among other things, prospects' e-mail addresses. Once you have this data base, you can target e-mail, fax broadcasts, direct mail, and other repeat promotions at them as appropriate.

It isn't difficult to get qualified prospects to "register" (fill out your enrollment page). You simply offer them something of value, which they cannot gain access to until they have completely filled out an enrollment page. This can be the ability to —

(a) download or request free literature,

(b) use an on-line calculator, search engine, or other Web site utility,

(c) subscribe to an e-mail newsletter or other on-line or printed publication, or

(d) request a price quotation or get some preliminary recommendations.

The principle is similar to that used in printed direct mail, which includes a reply card the advertiser wants the reader to fill out and mail back. Direct mail reply cards are filled out and returned only when the prospects are given an incentive to do so; when they are offered a free gift, free catalogue, free estimate, and so on. An enrollment page works exactly the same way. Give your site visitors a compelling reason to fill it out and they will.

9. Add functionality, not just information

Because Web pages are computer files run on computer systems, they can go beyond the regular printed page to offer degrees of functionality conventional sales literature cannot match.

For instance, on the home page for Studebaker-Worthington, a nationwide computer leasing company, there is a handy "Quick Quote" calculator you can access. You enter the purchase price of the computer system you are interested in and the calculator shows you the monthly lease payments.

On the home page for Edith Roman Associates, a large mailing list broker, there is a "Quick Count" calculator you can use to get instant list counts. You enter the type of market you want to reach; the program displays the names of the available mailing lists, the quantity of names on each list, and the list rental cost. This is a convenient feature for marketing managers who are planning campaigns and need to get a quick idea of the size of potential markets.

If your product or service lends itself to this type of calculator, add it to your Web site and make it accessible from your home page. You don't need to make it elaborate or have many extras like this. But adding a utility makes your Web site more interesting and useful, so more prospects will visit it more often.

10. Change the content periodically

Another big difference between printed brochures and on-line marketing documents is that on-line documents can easily be updated, at any time, with virtually no cost. Brochures, by comparison, cannot be updated once printed. If you have new information, you either have to reprint the brochure and throw out the old copies, or add an insert sheet or other supplement highlighting the new information (which doesn't delete any dated or wrong information in the old brochure).

Advertisers with Web sites find this flexibility to be a blessing and a burden. The blessing is that on-line marketing documents can always be up-to-date and don't cost anything to revise. The burden is that you're always going back into your Web site to make changes, revisions, and corrections as new information becomes available.

If the content of your Web site is being continually changed and upgraded, let your prospects know there is a reason to revisit your Web site periodically to obtain the latest, most accurate information. You can put a message on your home page that says: "Information changes rapidly and the XYZ Company Web Site is continually updated. Visit us often to get the most current data."

Another technique is to have a separate section or Web page dedicated specifically to news and announcements. This bulletin can change monthly, weekly, even daily. The more often it changes and the more important the information, the more frequently prospects will visit your site. If you have such an announcements page, feature it on your home page with a hypertext link and encourage browsers to visit it on every trip to your site.

11. Use a FAQ

FAQ stands for "frequently asked questions." A FAQ is a unique type of Web page containing questions and answers about your company and product. These pages are extremely important, very popular, and nearly always read. A FAQ is a way to convey information simply, easily, and quickly. If it weren't for your FAQ, your e-mail would be jammed with people asking the same questions over and over again.

A FAQ page at your Web site can be valuable. When people ask you questions, refer them to your FAQ. When people want to know more about what you do, point to your FAQ. When you receive e-mail requests for an information brochure, e-mail them your FAQ. Since the FAQ is a separate Web page, Web surfers can easily download it, and even print it for permanent reference.

Joe Vitale, an authority on Internet writing, offers these suggestions for writing effective FAQs:

(a) **Use the Q&A format.** FAQs rely on the tried-and-true question and answer format because that is the simplest way to get information across. If you've been around for a while, you've heard the same questions asked numerous times. These are the questions to include in your FAQ. Naturally, your succinct answers are included, too.

(b) **Be brief.** By now you know that everything you write on-line should be as brief and to the point as possible. There's too much happening on-line and too many other posts to read for anyone to spend a great deal of time on your material. Write a clear question, give a direct answer, and move on to the next question. Ten lines of text seems like a wise target for each of your answers.

(c) **Be lively.** FAQs that merely give facts can be boring. Spice up your writing. Add eye-opening statistics, engaging stories, stimulating quotes. Make reading your FAQ a delight. Say something that surprises your readers. Add a fact that makes them sit up and say, "I didn't know that!"

(d) **Give resources.** Although you aren't writing a term paper or dissertation, your FAQ is a resource for people. Make it a complete one by including details on how to get more information about your product or service. If you have a list of products for sale, include it. If you have a directory of people or departments for people to contact for more information, include it. And remember to add your own name, address, phone and fax numbers, and, of course, e-mail address.

(e) **List questions up front.** It's common practice to list all the questions being answered in your FAQ at the beginning of the FAQ. This way, anyone wanting to know the answer to a particular question can tell at a glance whether you cover it or not.

12. Cross-promote

Once you have a Web site, promote it heavily. In your ads, mailings, and company newsletter, encourage prospects and customers to visit your Web site. Put your Web site address (e.g., *http://www.bly.com*) on every marketing and business document you produce, including letterhead and business cards.

In marketing communications, include a benefit the prospect will receive as an incentive to go to your Web site. For instance, you may have special information that is available only on the Web site and not in other media. Or you may post special sales and discounts on the Web site that are available only on the site.

Studebaker-Worthington Leasing Corporation offers cash incentives and gifts of merchandise, available only on the Web site, to computer stores that use their leasing services. These special gifts increase their Internet traffic.

13. Use selective Web publishing

A basic Web site has a home page and a brief, one-page, Web page. But you have a lot more information about your products and services than can fit in these formats. What do you do?

You have two choices. As discussed in section **8.**, you can have an enrollment page where people browsing your Web site can register and request additional materials be sent to them via e-mail, fax, or *snail mail* (the Internet user's derogatory term for regular post office mail).

The alternative is to engage in *Web publishing*. In Web publishing, you convert marketing and informational documents to electronic form and place these electronic files on your Web server. The documents can then be read on-line, instantly downloaded, even printed out by browsers visiting your Web site.

Enrollment page response offers and Web publishing are not mutually exclusive. I recommend you put your most important marketing documents — those containing information most relevant and interesting to prospects — directly on your server so interested prospects can download them right from the Web.

But if you put all your documents on-line, you can clutter up your site and eat up your server space, so documents of secondary importance should be listed or described within the Web site and offered on the enrollment page. As a rule of thumb, the 10% most important marketing documents should be published on the Web site, with other relevant documents offered on the site through the enrollment page, e-mail, or other means.

14. Keep graphics to a minimum

Says Joe Vitale, "Don't overdo the graphics. Not everyone can see graphics on-line. Even those who can usually don't have the patience to download large graphic files. If users have slow modems, waiting for a graphic to appear on their screens might take several minutes . . . time for which some are being charged by their access provider or phone company. Use graphics selectively. Don't get fancy."

Graphics add interest, but words communicate the bulk of the information on the Internet. So keep your Web site simple. "Ease of communication and clarity of use should be your targets," says Vitale. "Always aim for simplicity. If your copywriting isn't compelling, few will buy. True, on-line browsers certainly want information, but don't feed it to them in dry chunks. The more you can add emotional excitement to your words, the better your chances of being read, being remembered, and having your services bought."

Vary what you write. Some people create their own paperless documents, such as *e-zines* (electronic magazines), and design them for home-page use. There are far too many diversions for readers in cyberspace, so don't bore anybody. With one click a reader can leave your site and never return.

Keep what you say interesting. Always think of your readers and give them what they want, not what you want. A good rule when writing any marketing piece is, "Get out of your ego and into the reader's ego."

As Howard Gossage, a famous ad executive, once said, "People read whatever interests them, and sometimes it's an ad." Make your on-line text interesting and they just might read what you write.

Be sure you place your name, address, phone and fax numbers, and e-mail address on every page of your Web site documents. You never know when a reader will suddenly want to contact you. Don't make that person backtrack through several layers of hypertext links just to find out your phone number. Put your contact information at the top of every page.

12

BIG PROFITS FROM PUBLIC RELATIONS

Publicity can generate enormous sales with a minimal investment. Sometimes press releases can be very profitable. I once generated more than $21,000 in front-end sales alone from a press release mailing costing under $600 (the release is reprinted later on in this chapter).

Publicity is news. If a press release is used by the media, it will be because it contains news of interest to a number of readers or listeners, not because it is meant to persuade readers or listeners to buy something.

Most people don't realize many of the news stories appearing in the media have been generated by press releases. News directors and editors can't possibly cover every story in person, so they rely on press releases to generate ideas for articles.

By alerting the media to newsworthy events, products, services, and people, you can prompt a newspaper, radio, or TV station to cover anything from the opening of a new restaurant to the publication of a new catalogue, from the techniques of an acupuncturist to the makings of a new trend.

In most cases, publicity supplements, rather than replaces, print advertising, but it's valuable enough that you should learn what a press release is, how it should be formatted, how to organize and write one, and some rules for effective style.

a. USE PROPER PRESS RELEASE FORMAT

A press release is a short article sent to the media in the hope of gaining publicity. Press releases are formatted in a way that makes them easily identifiable, and they are organized in a way that makes them easy for editors to edit (see section **b.**).

There are certain common elements of press release format. First, press releases are typed or word-processed — never handwritten. The name of the company releasing the information and a contact phone number are mentioned prominently at the top. The words "For immediate release," "Release at your convenience," or "Release date: XX, 19—" appear several lines under the company name and several lines above the headline.

If the release is being submitted beyond your locality, put a "dateline" before the first sentence of your release. The dateline consists of the city in capitals and the state or country in lower case — but no date (e.g., New York, NY).

Your release should be double-spaced on one side of a white 8½-by-11-inch piece of paper with wide margins and a headline in caps or boldface. If your press release's copy runs to more than one page, put

"MORE" (centered) at the bottom of each page except the final page.

Put a number "2" on the upper right-hand corner of the second page of the release. Succeeding pages are similarly numbered. At the bottom of the last page of the release, type ### or -30- to indicate the end of the release.

b. ORGANIZE YOUR RELEASE USING THE INVERTED PYRAMID STYLE

A press release is usually made up of a headline, a lead, and the body of the story. Like most news stories, press releases must get to the point quickly, be sufficiently newsworthy to interest a large segment of the media's audience, and be attention-catching enough to entice editors to run them.

Headlines must be concise and present the most significant or relevant point of the story in an attention-grabbing fashion. They are the store-window display of your news release. They summarize what is in the body copy and catch the reader's attention, all in two lines, maximum. Here are some effective press release headlines:

```
NEW POSTER COMBATS
SEXISM IN THE WORKPLACE
```
(A story about a poster on sexist terms)

```
TAPPING THE 'ELF' IN
'SELF' HELPS COMPANIES
BUILD TEAM SPIRIT, MO-
RALE, AND CREATIVITY
WHILE REDUCING STRESS
```

(A story about a new seminar on humor in the workplace)

```
ABBONDANZA, NEW YORK'S
FIRST 'ROSTICCERIA,'
OPENS ON UPPER EAST SIDE
— ABUNDANT DELICACIES
WITH AN ITALIAN ACCENT
```
(A story about a new Italian gourmet store)

```
PHOTOGRAPHY EXHIBITION
EVOKES OLANA, HOME OF
AMERICA'S GREATEST LAND-
SCAPE ARTIST, FREDERIC
CHURCHA
```
(Photography exhibit)

A press release's lead should include the who, what, when, where, and often the how and why of the story.

In a news story, journalists traditionally write with the "inverted pyramid" in mind. Their first paragraph summarizes the whole story. Succeeding paragraphs are progressively less vital. Therefore, if an editor needs to cut a story, he or she can cut from the bottom, knowing that even if only the first paragraph stays intact, the story will be told.

In any case, keep the lead short — large blocks of type intimidate or bore the reader.

c. FIND A HOOK OR ANGLE FOR YOUR RELEASE

Your release will attract more attention if you have a special hook or angle. The opening of a one-artist show could commemorate the artist's birth or death, for example. The release can then use the occasion as a way of promoting the exhibit. For a release on acupuncture, the publicist, trying to find a news hook, remembered it had been ten years since Nixon had renewed relations with China. The press release discussed acupuncture within the context of the changes in Chinese-American relations and cultural exchanges (see below).

An "angle" is a special way of viewing a topic. For example, a travel agency trying to promote trips to Paris chose to emphasize a tour of the Paris sewer systems in its release. It worked! The angle that has worked so well for the Maytag Company is that its appliances almost never break down. So we see the world of Maytag products through the eyes of a Maytag repairman ("the loneliest guy in town") who leads a lonely life of waiting to be called on to do a repair. If Maytag were to launch a campaign for pen pals for the Maytag repairman, it would be exploiting promotional possibilities based on the well-established angle of the TV commercials. For a press release on a new Italian gourmet store, the copywriter, looking for an original angle, used the little-known phrase "Rosticceria" (an Italian food store selling fresh-roasted meats) to help distinguish the gourmet store from dozens of similar gourmet take-out stores.

The style of a press release depends on the story and a copywriter's unique way of viewing that story. For a press release on the 20 most deadly phrases in business writing, you might use a humorous approach reminiscent of David Letterman's "Top 10" lists.

Quotations from people involved in the story give your release a liveliness and real-life flavor. In a press release written to promote an acupuncturist's practice ("TEN YEARS AFTER NORMALIZATION OF RELATIONS WITH CHINA, AMERICAN ACUPUNCTURE COMES OF AGE"), the acupuncturist summarized American attitudes toward acupuncture with a quote that was both colorful and that showed contrast, adding to the release's news interest:

> "Ten years ago, when you said 'acupuncture' to an American, he reacted as if you had said 'voodoo.' Today, millions of Americans visit acupuncturists for a variety of ills, and they do so with less fanfare — and a good deal less pain or anxiety — than when they visit their dentist," said Lo Sing, doctor of acupuncture.

Quotations not only support the story but, when attributed to real people, entice the editor to run the story.

d. AIMING YOUR RELEASE FOR THE MARKET

Learn everything you can about the publications to which you send your releases. Browse through copies of magazines or newspapers at your library or stationery store. See what types of stories are run and try to figure out where your story will fit. What are the space requirements? If you are looking to place news briefs, see if there's a section in the magazine that runs them. Note the names of the editors who watch over those sections. For newspapers, be aware of when they are published (daily, weekly) and see how that influences the chances of their running your story.

For radio and TV, you will send releases to either the news or talk show's managing editor or assignment editor. To gain the attention of a TV producer, you may have to include a videotape, photographs, or other evidence that the story is universal, timely, important, and visual.

If an editor or reporter believes your release is an attempt to get free advertising, your story will never get printed. Put news in each news release you write. Releases must contain a message of value to the publication's readers.

While trade journals will often publish stories weeks or even months old, the time limitations of TV, radio, and daily newspapers favor events that have an immediacy to readers.

Certain stories, known in publishing as "evergreens" (e.g., stories about Christmas sales, Groundhog Day, New Year's resolutions, end-of-year business wrap-ups), have a timeless quality and might well be slotted to run months or even years after they are sent to a particular magazine.

e. MODEL PRESS RELEASES

Samples #9 to #13 show several press releases in the standard format. Each was picked up as a medium- to feature-length article in one or more major magazines or newspapers. Most resulted in publicity in a dozen or more periodicals.

Sample #9 is a two-page press release I used to promote a booklet called "Recession Proof Business Strategies." I charged $7 for my booklet. This press release was sent to several hundred publications, including business magazines, syndicated business columnists, and business editors at large daily newspapers during the height of the recession of the early 1990s.

I chose to send each editor a copy of the booklet along with the press release because I felt it was impressive and would catch the editor's attention. However, it is not necessary to include your booklet to get the editor to use such a release, and because it's expensive to mail booklets with press releases, I normally don't do it.

This press release was picked up in dozens of publications. Some ran very short blurbs from the press release, others ran the release almost word for word. The release generated sales of more than 3,000 booklets at $7 each.

FROM: Bob Bly, 174 Holland Avenue, New Milford, NJ 07646

CONTACT: Bob Bly (201) 385-1220

For immediate release

NEW BOOKLET REVEALS 14 PROVEN STRATEGIES FOR KEEPING BUSI-NESSES BOOMING IN A BUST ECONOMY

New Milford, NJ — While some companies struggle to survive in today's sluggish business environment, many are doing better than ever largely because they have mastered the proven but little known strategies of "recession marketing."

That's the opinion of Bob Bly, an independent marketing consultant and author of the just-published booklet, "Recession Proof Business Strategies: 14 Winning Methods to Sell Any Product or Service in a Down Economy."

"Many business people fear a recession or soft economy, because when the economy is weak, their clients and customers cut back on spending," says Bly. "To survive in such a marketplace, you need to develop recession marketing strategies that help you retain your current accounts and keep those customers buying. You also need to master marketing techniques that will win you new clients or customers to replace any business you may have lost because of the increased competition that is typical of a recession."

Among the recession-fighting business strategies Bly outlines in his new booklet:

- Reactivate dormant accounts. An easy way to get more business is to call past clients or customers people you served at one time but are not actively working for now — to remind them of your existence. According to Bly, a properly scripted telephone call to a list of past buyers will generate approximately one order for every ten calls.

- Quote reasonable affordable fees and prices in competitive bid situations. While you need not reduce your rates or prices, in competitive bid situations you will win by bidding toward the low end or middle of your price range rather than at the high end. Bly says that during a recession, your bids should be 15 to 20 percent lower than you would normally charge in a healthy economy.

MORE

2

- <u>Give your existing clients and customers a superior level of service</u>. In a recession, Bly advises businesses to do everything they can to hold onto their existing clients or customers. "The best way to hold onto your clients or customers is to please them," says Bly, "and the best way to please them is through better customer service. Now is an ideal time to provide that little bit of extra service or courtesy that can mean the difference between dazzling the client or customer and merely satisfying them."

- <u>Reactivate old leads</u>. Most businesses give up on sales leads too early, says Bly. He cites a study from Thomas Publishing that found that although 80 percent of sales to businesses are made on the fifth call, only one out of ten salespeople calls beyond three times. Concludes Bly: "You have probably not followed up on leads diligently enough, and the new business you need may already be right in your prospect files." He says repeated follow-up should convert 10 percent of prospects to buyers.

To receive a copy of Bly's booklet, "Recession Proof Business Strategies," send $8 ($7 plus $1 shipping and handling) to: Bob Bly, Dept. 109, 174 Holland Avenue, New Milford, NJ 07646. Cash, money orders, and checks (payable to "Bob Bly") accepted. (Add $1 for Canadian orders.)

Bob Bly, an independent copywriter and consultant based in New Milford, NJ, specializes in business-to-business, hi-tech, and direct-response marketing. He is the author of 18 books, including <u>How To Promote Your Own Business</u> (New American Library) and <u>The Copywriter's Handbook</u> (Henry Holt). A frequent speaker and seminar leader, Mr. Bly speaks nationwide on the topic of how to market successfully in a recession or soft economy.

# # #

SAMPLE #10
PRESS RELEASE

FROM: PLATO Software, 3158 Rt. 9W, Saugerties, NY 12477

CONTACT: Richard Rosen, phone 914-246-6648

For immediate release

NEW ACCOUNTING SOFTWARE PACKAGE HAS UNIQUE FEATURE: CAN BE MODIFIED BY USERS TO FIT THEIR BUSINESS PROCEDURES AND OPERATIONS

Saugerties, NY — PLATO Software has just released the new version of its modifiable business and accounting software package, P&L-Pro Version 2.0.

What makes P&L-Pro unique is that it's the only affordably priced accounting software that can be modified by the user with no programming required, claims Richard Rosen, president, PLATO Software.

"Most low-end, off-the-shelf business software forces you to adjust your business procedures to accommodate the limitations of the program," says Rosen. "As a result, you cannot get the software to do things your way. Some high-end business software packages are designed to be modifiable, but these start at $5,000 to $7,000 and up for a complete system."

P&L-Pro, by comparison, is a complete and affordably priced business and accounting software package that can be modified by users, even nonprogrammers, to precisely fit their procedures and operations. Cost is approximately $100 per module.

How P&L-Pro works:

Most business software, according to Rosen, is created using complex programming languages, and therefore can only be altered by computer programmers.

P&L-Pro, however, was built using Alpha Four, an easy-to-use database management system. As a result, users can add functions to or modify their copies of P&L-Pro directly, without help from a programmer or software consultant.

MORE

2

The new version, P&L-Pro 2.0, features faster General Ledger posting, simplified set-up, better-looking screens, and optimized performance. It also includes two new modules, Payroll and Inventory Control, which — added to the existing modules of General Ledger, Accounts Receivable, and Accounts Payable — make P&L-Pro a complete business and accounting software package that is fully modifiable by the user.

The Payroll module includes all state and federal tax tables and features multiple pay types, unlimited deduction types, and time-card entry. It is completely interfaced with the P&L-Pro General Ledger module. A special feature enables the user to print checks for the new year while still being able to print W-2 forms for the prior year.

The Inventory Control module generates an unlimited number of sales and inventory reports. These reports give the user an up-to-the-minute picture of inventory by product, stock number, location, or any other criteria selected. The module handles purchase order entry, receiving, sales order entry, and shipping. And it can be easily customized to fit any method of inventory management and control.

P&L-Pro 2.0 with all five modules sells for $495. A nonmodifiable version is available for $249. To order or for more information contact: PLATO Software, 3158 Route 9W, Saugerties, NY 12477, phone 800-SWPLATO (800-797-5286), fax 914-246-7597.

# # #

FROM: Brookdale International Systems Inc., Vancouver, B.C.

CONTACT: Ernest Moniz, phone (604) 324-3822

For immediate release

NEW FREE BOOKLET OUTLINES FIRE SAFETY TIPS FOR FAMILIES

8-point Family Escape Plan Can Help Save Lives, says Booklet Author

Vancouver, B.C. — If there's a fire in your home, you and your family have a better chance of getting out safely if you develop an escape plan and practice it on a regular basis.

This advice and other fire safety tips are presented in a new, free booklet, "How to Make Your Family Safer From Fires," published by Brookdale International Systems, manufacturer of the EVAC.U8 Emergency Escape Smoke Hood. The booklet is available free of charge to the general public.

"To have a good fire safety program, you must develop a family escape plan and practice it with your entire family, including small children," says John Swann, president of the firm and author of the booklet. "Go over the escape plan, have fire drills every 6 months, and teach children that they must be prepared to leave the home by themselves if necessary."

The booklet presents an 8-step escape plan families can use and teach to their own children. Among the fire safety tips covered:

- Check the door to see if the exit is safe. Brace your foot up against the door so that it cannot open more than an inch. If there is smoke, heat, or fire on the other side, use an alternate exit.

- Make sure alternate exits exist. Draw a floor plan of your home, and find two ways to get out of each room. There should be at least one way to get out of each bedroom without opening the door.

- Stay close to the floor and crawl if necessary. Smoke and hot gases rise.

MORE

2

- Get and learn how to use fire safety equipment such as smoke alarms, fire extinguishers, and emergency smoke hoods. Smoke alarms should be installed in each bedroom and each level of the home according to fire codes.

- Decide on a meeting place where family members will meet a safe distance from your home after exiting the house. Make sure children understand they should go there and wait for you in case of fire. Never go back inside a burning building.

- Eliminate fire hazards in the home. Keep all exit routes and stairwells free from obstructions at all time.

Brookdale International Systems Inc. manufactures and markets the EVAC-U8 Emergency Escape Smoke Hood throughout North America. The EVAC-U8 is a portable breathing hood designed to protect family members from smoke inhalation while evacuating a burning building.

Fire death statistics in North America show that 3 out of 4 people who die in fires succumb to smoke inhalation. Proper use of the EVAC-U8 emergency smoke hood prevents toxic fumes from overcoming the wearer, allowing him or her to stay conscious and mobile to escape from a lethal, smoke-filled environment.

Each EVAC-U8 smoke hood is attached to a lightweight, compact multi-stage chemical catalytic filter that removes carbon monoxide, other fumes, and particulates to purify the air which is breathed through a mouthpiece. The system has a shelf life of 5 years.

In his book, _Collision Course_, consumer activist Ralph Nader recommends the use of smoke hoods. The EVAC-U8 hood was recently featured on CNN. More than 30,000 have been sold in North America.

For a free copy of the "How to Make Your Family Safer from Fires" booklet of fire safety tips, call or write: Brookdale International, 1-8755 Ash Street, Vancouver, B.C., Canada V6P 6T3, phone (604) 324-3822, fax (604) 324-3821. To order EVAC-U8, send check or money order for $64 ($59.95 plus $4.05 shipping and handling, payable to "Brookdale International") to the above address.

— 30 —

FROM: Echols International Tourism Institute, 660 LaSalle Place, Highland Park, IL 60035

CONTACT: Stacy L. Goldstin, Director of Student Services, 708-266-7575

<u>For immediate release</u>

NEW FREE BOOKLET EDUCATES RECENT GRADUATES, JOB SEEKERS, AND CAREER CHANGERS ON OPPORTUNITIES IN THE TRAVEL INDUSTRY

Chicago, IL — Are you sick and tired of your job? Do you dream of a career that's fun, exciting — and financially rewarding? Do you desire to go on vacations, travel to exotic locations, or see the world? And would you like to travel for free?

If so, "a career in the travel industry is an option you should seriously investigate," says Stacy Goldstin, Director of Student Services, Echols International Tourism Institute, a school providing job training for people who want to break into the field.

To help job seekers make an informed career decision, Echols has recently published a 16-page booklet, "Career Opportunities In Today's Travel Industry." It outlines opportunities for employment with travel agencies, hotels, airlines, tour companies, cruise lines, convention centers, car rental companies, and other travel-related companies.

For a limited time, Echols is giving away the booklet free of charge to anyone who requests a copy by calling toll-free 800-827-2051 or writing them at their Highland Park, IL offices.

Goldstin says the travel business is the world's largest provider of jobs and the fastest-growing industry. Annual travel and tourism revenues worldwide exceed $3 trillion, and one out of every nine jobs is in a travel-related profession.

According to the Echols booklet, in the United States the travel industry is the second largest employer overall, and the number-one employer in 37 of the 50 states. It employs 6 million Americans directly and millions more in related jobs.

Other facts revealed in the booklet:

- Travel and tourism is the leading export of the United States.

MORE

2

- On a global scale, the travel industry creates a new job every ten seconds.
- The American Society of Travel Agents reports that travel and tourism is the third largest retail industry in the world in terms of gross income.

$25,000+ annual income

As described in the free booklet, experienced travel agents can earn $25,300 to $36,000 a year or more, and other travel-industry positions can pay even better: Tour guides, for example, can earn up to $65,000 a year.

In addition, travel professionals receive many perks. These include free travel to exotic locations, luxury cruises for only $25 a day, 75% discounts on air travel, and half-off regular room rates at hotels worldwide. Flight attendants, for example, can fly free on their own airline.

Founded in 1962, the Echols International Travel & Hotel Schools have trained more than 12,800 students for careers in the travel and hotel industries. More than 90 percent of these students have gotten jobs in the travel field following graduation.

Now the Echols program is available in a convenient correspondence course for self-paced home study. The Echols International Tourism Institute Home Study Course for the Travel and Hotel Industries, which offers a travel diploma by mail, is described in detail in the free "Career Opportunities" booklet. Other topics covered in the booklet include advantages of travel industry careers, job opportunities, salaries and perks, job hunting tips, and financial aid available. There is also a self-scoring aptitude test to help readers determine whether they would enjoy a career in travel.

To request your free copy of "Career Opportunities in Travel," contact: Echols International Tourism Institute, 660 LaSalle Place, Highland Park, IL 60035, phone 800-827-2051.

EDITOR: Review copy of booklet available upon request. Call 708-266-7575 and ask for Stacy Goldstin

# # #

FROM: Remarkable Technologies, 245 Pegasus Ave., Northvale, NJ 07647

CONTACT: Jack Lahav or Rob Curtis, phone 201-767-5522

For immediate release

WRITING BUSINESS PLANS TO RAISE MONEY FOR YOUR SMALL BUSI-NESS USED TO COST A SMALL FORTUNE; NOW DO-IT-YOURSELF FOR UNDER $100

New business planning, budgeting, and forecasting PC software provides cost-effective alternative to high-priced business planning consulting services

Northvale, NJ — It's ironic: Many small businesses creating formal business plans write the plans primarily to raise capital from potential lenders or investors.

But hiring professional consultants to write these business plans has become a major business in itself, requiring a large outlay of capital that most of these small cash-strapped businesses don't have.

That's where Jack Lahav, president of Remarkable Technologies, stepped in. Realizing that the fees charged by many business-plan-writing services are beyond the reach of most of the small businesses that need plans written, his software company, Remarkable Technologies, has introduced a "do-it-yourself" software package for writing business plans — B-Plan for Windows.

With B-Plan, any business owner or manager sitting at a PC can write the best business plan in a few hours, claims Lahav. What's more, their only cost is the software, which sells for under $100!

Gives you what others charge a fortune for

"Business plan writers charge even small companies anywhere from $5,000 to $15,000 for a single plan," says Lahav. "That's outrageous, considering that much of what appears in the plans is 'boilerplate' text they copy from one plan to the next. It's not original material . . . but they charge as if each plan were wholly created from scratch."

MORE

122

2

For example, he tells of a Saugerties, NY, entrepreneur who recently paid a consulting firm $15,000 to write a plan his start-up company could use to raise capital. "And when he got the plan, it wasn't what he wanted and he wasn't happy with the quality of the work," says Lahav.

B-Plan automates much of the writing and financial calculations involved in creating a business plan, saving time and money. Small business owners have greater control over their plan when they write it themselves, using B-Plan. They also avoid the frustration of having to explain their complex business ideas to outside writers.

Another plus of using B-Plan is that the business plan is an easily modifiable computer file. "This makes it a living, working document that can be referenced on-line and modified as business conditions change. When the plan is written by someone else, it usually gathers dust on the shelf and is soon forgotten," observes Lahav.

Also, B-Plan enables the user to write as many different plans as needed with no extra charges.

3 steps to a better business plan

Creating a business plan with B-Plan is a simple 3-step process. First, the user enters key business data including sales plans, profit margins, budget, expenses, plants and equipment, and capital sources. The program provides simple fill-in-the-blank forms and tables for entering this data. Extensive business knowledge and computer skills are not required. "You don't have to be an accountant or computer programmer to use B-Plan," says Lahav.

Once a business's data is entered, B-Plan performs the necessary financial analysis at the touch of a key, including profit-and-loss projections, cash flow projections, break-even analysis reports, and projected balance sheets. All reports can be presented in text and graphic form.

MORE

123

3

Finally, B-Plan generates a complete written business plan, including the financial data, graphics, and text. An easy-to-follow fill-in template provides all the proper headings for a standard business plan. These include executive summary, company history, products and services, market analysis, marketing strategy, research and development plan, management, organization, operational plan, facilities, equipment, and financial plan. In addition, the program shows you exactly where to incorporate your B-Plan data, reports, and projections within the text, making the plan truly customized.

B-Plan requires an IBM 386 or higher (or 100% compatible) with 4 MB of RAM running Windows 3.1 or higher. Also required are a hard disk drive with 4 MB available, a mouse, EGA or higher resolution monitor (recommended), and MS-DOS 3.3 or higher.

B-Plan is not available in computer stores and must be ordered from Remarkable Technologies direct. To order call toll-free 800-782-1955 or send $104.95 ($99.95 plus $5 shipping and handling) to: Remarkable Technologies, 245 Pegasus Avenue, Northvale, NJ 07647, fax 201-767-7227. American Express, Visa, MasterCard accepted. The product comes with a 30-day money back guarantee. Remarkable Technologies is a leading marketer of business productivity software for the PC.

EDITOR: For a free review copy of B-Plan call Rob Curtis (201) 767-5522

# # #

13

CATALOGUES AND MINI-CATALOGUES

a. WHY DO CUSTOMERS BUY FROM CATALOGUES?

Catalogues are sales tools, designed to generate either leads or direct sales. To write catalogue copy that sells, you need to understand the reasons why customers buy from catalogues.

1. To save money

Saving money is the number one motivation for a buyer to order your product instead of your competitor's. Your catalogue should stress cost savings — on the cover, on the order form, on every page.

In Radio Shack's catalogues, every item is on sale. Each item description lists three things: the price off (in dollars or percentage), the regular price, and the sale price.

A catalogue from Boardroom Books shows a markdown on every book in the catalogue; the original price is crossed out with an X and the new price is printed next to it in red type.

An office supply catalogue from Business Envelope Manufacturers announces "Lowest Prices in the Industry" right on the front cover.

2. To be right

Buyers want to be sure they are buying the right product from the right vendor. How do you assure buyers they are making the right decision? Here are a few specific techniques:

- List well-known firms that have done business with you.

- Use testimonials. Pepper your catalogue with quotations from satisfied customers who praise your products.

- Make a guarantee. Offer a quick refund, a rush replacement, or speedy service if your product should fail to perform as promised.

- Give facts that demonstrate the stability of your company: years in the business, number of employees, number of locations, annual sales.

3. To make money

Business customers buy products for one of two end uses: to resell the products at a profit or to use them to operate their business more efficiently and profitably. Many consumer mail order catalogue products are designed to help the buyer save or make money.

Catalogue copy should show readers how they can make money by doing business with you. For example, "Telephone selling skills that increase sales" is a better headline than "Fundamentals of telephone sales." The first headline promises wealth; the second is merely descriptive.

4. To get something for nothing

Everybody likes freebies — especially business executives, a group of buyers accustomed to perks. Your catalogue could offer the buyer a free gift in exchange for an order. This should be a personal gift for the buyer, not a discount or gift of merchandise to the company.

Popular gift items for business executives include pen-and-pencil sets, clocks, calculators, mugs, ties, golf balls, T-shirts, and watches. (A warning: certain industries, such as defense and aerospace manufacturing, frown on this practice. To be safe, don't offer a premium worth more than $10.)

5. To fulfill a need

To the purchasing agent, whose job it is to buy things for a company, a good catalogue is a valuable sourcebook of much-needed merchandise. The more the catalogue and its contents fulfill his or her needs, the more likely the purchasing agent is to order from it — again and again.

How do you create a catalogue that fulfills the buyer's needs? First, find out what those needs are and fill the catalogue with products that satisfy them. Next, make sure your product list is broad enough. Otherwise, the buyer will be forced to turn to your competitor's catalogue for help. Be sure to include a wide variety of models, sizes, colors, and styles. Also, feature your most popular or hard-to-get items near the front of the book.

6. To solve problems

Often, the buyer isn't looking for a specific product. Rather, he or she is looking for a solution to a problem. If your catalogue shows how your product solves the problem, you'll make the sale.

For example, a plant manager might not be thinking of ultrafiltration. He or she might not even know what it is. But the headline, "The Smoothflow Ultrafilter Removes 99% of Dispersed Oil from Plant Wastewater" immediately alerts the manager that ultrafiltration can solve the plant's oily wastewater problem.

7. Other reasons

Other reasons why people buy from catalogues: to save time, for convenience, to feel important, to gratify curiosity, to take advantage of opportunities, to avoid effort, to make work easier, to avoid embarrassment, to be the first to try a new product or service, to be exclusive, to avoid salespeople. Keep these reasons in mind and gear your catalogue toward their fulfillment. It's a good way to make sure the customer orders from your catalogue instead of your competitor's.

b. TEN WAYS TO ORGANIZE YOUR CATALOGUE

1. By product demand

You can organize your catalogue by the sales each product generates. Put your bestsellers up front and give them a full page or half page each. Slower moving merchandise appears at the back of the book with a quarter page or less. Dead items are dropped altogether.

This organizational technique follows a principle first articulated by David Ogilvy: "Back your winners and abandon your losers." It puts your promotional dollars where they'll do the most good. But be careful. In large or highly technical product catalogues, this organizational scheme may cause some confusion.

2. By application

The Faultless Division of Axia Incorporated organized its caster catalogue by application. The catalogue has casters for general duty, light duty, light-medium duty up to heavy duty, textiles, scaffolds, floor trucks, and furniture.

Organizing according to application makes it easy for your customer to find the product that solves his or her problem. The disadvantage of this scheme is redundancy: many products handle multiple applications and must be listed (or cross-referenced) in more than one section.

3. By function

A software catalogue can be organized by the function each program performs: word processing, financial analysis, data base management, accounting, inventory, graphics, communications. Obviously, this scheme won't work in a catalogue where all the equipment performs the same task (e.g., a catalogue of pollution-control equipment or safety valves).

4. By type of equipment

Radio Shack's consumer electronics catalogues are organized by product group: stereos on one page, car radios on the next, followed by VCRs, computers, and tape recorders. This scheme is a natural for companies that carry multiple product lines.

5. By system hierarchy

This technique organizes by the level at which each component fits into the overall system. For example, if you manufacture computer hardware, your catalogue can begin with the turnkey systems you offer.

Next come the major components: terminals, printers, plotters, disk drives, keyboards, processors. Then you get to the board level, showing the various optional circuit boards you offer for memory expansion, interfaces, communications, instrument control, and other functions. Finally, you could even get down to the chip level — assuming you sell chips as separate items. Supplies — paper, printer ribbons, diskettes, instruction manuals — would go in a separate section at the end of the catalogue. This unit/sub unit/sub-sub unit approach is ideal for manufacturers who sell both complete systems and component parts.

6. By price

If you sell similar products that vary mainly in quality and price, you can organize your catalogue by selling price. If your customers are concerned with savings, start with the cheapest items and work up. If you're selling to an upscale group willing to pay a premium for the deluxe model, start with high-priced versions and work down.

This is an excellent technique for organizing a catalogue of premiums and incentives. After all, an ad manager searching for a premium has a price range in mind, not necessarily a specific product. Make it easy for him or her to find the $1 giveaways as well as the $50 executive gifts.

7. By scarcity

If your catalogue features hard-to-get items, consider putting them up front, even on the cover. This makes your catalogue more valuable by offering buyers products they need but can't get anywhere else. Don't worry that these hard-to-find items aren't big sellers. When customers know your catalogue has a stock of rare merchandise (and they use your catalogue to order it), they'll be more inclined to do other business with you, too.

8. By size

If you make one product and the basic selection criterion is size, it's natural to organize your catalogue by size (dimensions, weight, horsepower, BTUs, or whatever). This is handy for catalogues with boilers, motors, shipping drums, envelopes, light bulbs, air conditioners, and other equipment selected primarily on a size basis.

9. By model number

If you've worked out a sensible numbering system for your product line, organize your catalogue by model number. If there's a simple meaning to your numbering system, explain it at the start of the catalogue. And don't rely solely on the model numbers to describe your products; include headings and descriptive text as well.

10. Alphabetically

If no other system works for you, you can always organize alphabetically. A large tool catalogue can start with adjustable strap clamps and angle plates and end with wing nuts and wrenches. Or a vitamin catalogue can start with Vitamin A and end with Zinc.

c. A GOOD CATALOGUE TELLS AND SELLS WITH COPY BASICS

The following fundamentals of catalogue copywriting can add to the pulling power of your next mailing.

(a) **Use colorful, descriptive language.** Product specs and tech talk don't move buyers to action. Persuasive language does. It's colorful and descriptive, painting a picture in readers'

minds of what the product can do for them. For example:

Tech-talk: "The XYZ mixer is devoid of pinch-points or dead spots where viscous material might accumulate."

Persuasive language: "Our mixer is free of sharp edges, nooks, and crannies where gunk might get stuck and clog up your pipeline."

(b) **Use precise language.** Beware of language that is overly colloquial or general. You want your writing to be conversational enough to win the reader over without becoming so vague that it doesn't communicate your meaning. For example, an ad for a microwave relay system began with the headline, "If you thought microwaves are too rich for your blood, look again." At first glance, one might think the ad has something to do with the danger of microwave radiation and blood poisoning. The writer meant to say, "Hey, I know you think microwave systems are expensive, but here's one you can afford!" More precise language is needed here, something like, "At last . . . an affordable microwave system for cable TV operators."

(c) **Use specific language.** Recently, a Hollywood screenwriter spoke about the secret to her success in writing major feature films. "Specifics sell. When you are abstract, no one pays attention." And so it is with the catalogue writer: specifics sell. Generalities don't. A lazy copywriter might write:

```
Key to a successful
chemical plant is equip-
ment that works — without
problems or breakdowns.
And our gear drive works
and works and works — a
long, long time. Put it
in place, turn it on, and
forget about it. It's
that simple.
```

Sounds nice, but empty. Exactly how reliable is the gear drive? How long can it go without maintenance? What proof do you offer for your claims of superior reliability? This is what the buyer wants to know. So the skilled copywriter fills catalogue copy with specifics that give the answers:

```
Continuous internal lu-
bricating sprays keep
our gear drives well
oiled and virtually
friction free. As a re-
sult, there's no wear and
tear, and service life is
greatly increased. In
laboratory tests, our
system has operated
25,000 hours nonstop. In
the field, we have more
than 25,000 units in-
stalled and not a single
failure.
```

(d) **Use descriptive heads and breakers.** Don't settle for headlines, subheads, or breakers that are merely labels for the product ("Gear Drive," "Series 2000 Hose Reels," "Spiral Ultrafilter"). Instead, put some sell in your headlines. State a benefit. Promise to solve a problem. Mention the industries that can use the product. Tell its applications. Describe the range of sizes, colors, or models available. Give news about the product. Stress the ease of product evaluation and selection in your catalogue. Some examples:

- A Quick and Easy Guide to Hose Selection

- Widest Selection of Laboratory Stoppers from $\frac{1}{4}$ inch to 1 foot in diameter — rubber, plastic, glass, and cork

- Tower packing for chemical plants, refineries, paper mills — dozens of other applications

- Color-coded floppy diskettes save time and make your life easy! Here's the full story . . .

(e) **Make it easy to order.** If your catalogue is one of those monsters jammed with tables of product specs, be sure to explain these tables to your readers up front. Tell your readers what's in the tables and how to use them to select the product. Give simple procedures and formulas to aid in product selection. Illustrate with a few examples. Also, make sure your reader knows who to call for assistance or order placement.

(f) **Make it easy to read.** Use short, familiar words. Short sentences. Short paragraphs with space between each. Stick in underlines, bullets, boldface type, and breakers for emphasis. A catalogue crammed with technical data and tiny type is a bore and a strain on the eyes. You can make your business catalogue effective and yet fun and easy to read.

(g) **Stress benefits, benefits, benefits.** What the product does for the reader is more important than how it works, how you made it, who invented it, how long you've been making it, or how well it has sold.

1. How to determine the proper tone for your copy

"Catalogue copy should be brisk, concise, stripped-down prose," one expert told me. "Cram as many facts as you can. Use bullets, sentence fragments, word lists. Don't waste time with fancy sales talk; just pile on the description."

"Catalogue copy should talk to the reader, as one friend talking to another," says another expert. "Use conversational copy to build sales arguments that compel the reader to buy the product. The sales pitch — not a pile of product specifications — is what counts."

Should catalogue copy be in prose form or bullet form? Should it be clipped and concise or leisurely and conversational? Crammed with facts or written to entertain as well as educate? Although no two experts agree, here are some factors to help you determine the tone and style of your catalogue copy.

(a) **Space.** Space is obviously the greatest limitation. If you have only one column-inch per item, you've got to write lean, bare-bones, telegraphic copy. Write the basic facts and nothing more. If you have a full page per item, you have the luxury of writing a conversational, ad-style sales pitch on each product. Keep in mind, however, that length alone does not make copy better. Going on and on while saying nothing is not good selling copy. Also remember that a catalogue can have as many pages and items as you want it to, so if the product can't be adequately described in the space available, you should consider adding more pages.

(b) **The product.** The copy style varies according to the type of product being sold. A catalogue selling laboratory equipment naturally contains some highly technical language, while a catalogue of bridal accessories has a warm, friendly tone. The complexity of the product also affects the length of the copy; you can say more about a microprocessor than you can about a stick of chewing gum.

(c) **Purpose.** If the customer is going to order directly from the catalogue, it must have complete product information and technical specifications. Copy has to be clear, comprehensive, and to the point. A catalogue used as a sales aid can be more "salesy" and less all-encompassing than the direct-order catalogue. A promotional catalogue geared to whetting the customer's appetite will contain benefit-oriented headlines and subheads, highly sales-oriented copy, and sophisticated graphics to engage the reader's attention. Remember, however, that no matter what the purpose of your catalogue, not giving enough merchandise details can be a sales deterrent. A promotional catalogue lacking product facts may never stimulate the customer's interest.

(d) **The buyer.** How sophisticated is the buyer? How much does he or she already know about the product and its uses? How much more does he or she want to know? A paint catalogue aimed at professional painters need only describe the color, composition, and other features of the various paints. A catalogue selling paint to the consumer would have to provide more of an education in the basics: types of paints available, pros and cons of each, applications best suited to each kind of paint, and tips on how to apply paint.

(e) **The buyer/seller relationship.** If your buyers are already sold on your firm and have a tradition of doing business with you, your catalogue can be a simple, straightforward description of your latest offerings. On the other hand, prospects who don't know you and your firm will need to be convinced that they should do their business with you instead of with your competitor. A catalogue aimed at this type of buyer will have to do a lot more selling and company image-building. The type of relationship you wish to have with your customers will also affect the tone you use (warm and friendly, formal and highly professional, etc.).

(f) **Past experience.** Measure catalogue results to the best of your ability and try to learn from past experience. If

cutting copy from a full page of hard-selling prose to a terse quarter-page entry doesn't reduce sales, cut the copy and get more items per page. If increasing each item from a quarter page to a full page boosts sales 500%, consider expanding all entries to a full page and increasing the size of the catalogue.

Remember, every situation is different. In the final analysis, the best way to set the tone and length of your copy is to know what works with your market and your customer.

2. Should catalogue copy tell the truth?

No one pretends that catalogue copy (or any other promotional copy) is objective. Everyone knows copy is written to get people to buy the product. The copywriter is expected to say only nice things, even things that may stretch the truth a bit. But how far should one go in order to make the sale? Here are some guidelines:

(a) **Stress the positive.** You don't need to lie to sell. Every product has its good features. Dig to find them and highlight these points in copy. If you can't find enough positives, re-evaluate carrying the product.

(b) **Omit negatives.** Never bad-mouth your own product in catalogue copy. Stress the positive features; leave out the negatives. Don't feel compelled to discuss your product's problems. The competition will be glad to do that for you. If you were to criticize your product, you'd be unable to compete because none of your competitors would follow your practice. As a result, buyers would hear the negatives of your product but not of others — so they'd buy the other product. There are three exceptions to this rule:

(i) When everybody knows about a problem. In this case, since you can't avoid talking about it, you may as well bring it out in the open and deal with it.

(ii) When you've eliminated a problem. Talk about the problem and then immediately explain how you ended the problem or improved the product. This tactic turns a negative into a positive.

(iii) When the negative aspect is offset by an even greater positive. For example, a negative of your outdoor tool shed is that it's made of a cheap-looking aluminum instead of the attractive redwood used by the competition. But the positive is that the aluminum is lightweight, easy to install, never needs painting or other maintenance, won't rot and lasts a lifetime — unlike the wood.

(c) **Be specific.** Many catalogue marketers describe their product as "the fastest," "the lowest cost," "the most efficient," or "the best performer" when they don't really know how their product compares to others on the market. Don't make general statements you can't prove; you may be caught in a lie. Even if you aren't caught, buyers distrust general statements. Be specific. Say "loads the program in 2.5 seconds" or "price reduced to $495.95" or "detects moisture down to 3 parts per million." Make specific, true claims, and people will believe you.

(d) **Be honest, but err on the side of optimism.** Let's say you tested the reliability of your product. In 85 out of 100 tests, the product lasted 16 months before breaking down. In 5 tests it lasted longer (up to 17 months); in 9 tests it broke down sooner (in 14 or 15 months); and one tested sample lasted only 10 months. You can feel comfortable claiming your product "lasts up to 16 months." Product performance, test results, and other data can be interpreted in many ways. A catalogue marketer should interpret data honestly, but in the best light possible.

(e) **If you must weasel, be straightforward.** Your goal is to ship all orders within 48 hours, and usually you do. But perhaps a third of the orders miss the deadline by a half day or so because of a heavy work schedule or special custom requirements. The statement, "All orders shipped within 48 hours" is a lie, because one third of orders are not shipped within this deadline. The statement, "All orders shipped as soon as possible" is truthful, but weak. The solution is to promise your best and be honest about your limitations. For example:

```
We do our best to ship
your order within 48
hours, but occasionally
it takes an extra day if
our backlog is heavy or
```

your order requires special customized work. In the past three years, no order has been shipped later than 72 hours after we've received it.

(f) **Make promises you can keep.** Then keep them. One function of promotional copy is to motivate the company to live up to its advertising. In your copy it's okay to make promises you intend to keep. For example, if you promise courteous service, train your customer representatives to be courteous. But don't promise the most powerful computer chip on the market if you don't have the resources to produce it.

(g) **Never lie.** If you make a claim that is clearly a lie, you'll be caught. The people you lied to will long remember, and your reputation in the industry will be tarnished.

(h) **Check the truth of your statements.** If your catalogue copy claims, "Ordering is as easy as picking up the phone," you should try picking up the phone and ordering from your catalogue. If the grandiose promises and proclamations you make in your catalogue copy don't reflect reality, either change the copy or, preferably, improve your way of doing business.

3. Checklist for effective catalogue copy

Before you approve your catalogue copy and send it to the typesetter, you want to be sure that it's right. Getting it right involves more than the basics of spelling and punctuation. It involves more than avoiding superlatives and generalities about your merchandise. Here's a handy checklist to help you review your present copy. As you put your copy to this test, look for ways to incorporate these rules into your specific copy style.

(a) **Is your copy in the right order?** Is there a logical scheme to the presentation of copy points about your merchandise? And have you been faithful to this organizational principle throughout? Is this the best way to organize your items in your catalogue or would another method make more sense?

(b) **Is it persuasive?** Does your copy begin with a strong selling message? Have you used copy to indicate your sales message on the catalogue cover? Do individual headlines promise solutions to reader problems and draw the readers into the product descriptions? Does the body copy stress user benefits as well as technical features?

(c) **Is it complete?** If the catalogue is designed to generate direct sales, does it include all the information the reader needs to make a buying decision? Does it make it easy for the customer to specify and order the product? If the catalogue is designed to generate leads, does it contain enough information to interest qualified prospects? Does it encourage them to take the next step in the buying process? Have you described products fully? Have you included all important details such as size, operating efficiency, model numbers, equipment compatibility, materials of construction, accessories, and options?

(d) **Is it clear?** Is the copy understandable and easy to read? Are all technical terms defined, all abbreviations spelled out? Is it written at the reader's level of technical understanding?

(e) **Is it consistent?** Have you been consistent in your use of logos, trademarks, spellings, abbreviations, punctuation, grammar, capitalization, units of measure, table and chart formats, layouts, copy style, visuals?

(f) **Is it accurate?** Is the copy technically accurate? Has an engineer checked all numbers, specifications, and calculations to make sure they are correct? Have you carefully proofread tables, lists, and other fine print? Do the photos show the current models or versions of your product? Have you matched the right photo to each item description?

(g) **Is it interesting?** Is your catalogue attractive to look at, lively and informative to read? Or is it boring? The typeface you choose for your copy and the layout you use to display it encourage (or discourage) the viewer's desire to read the copy.

(h) **Is it believable?** Is the copy sincere or full of ballyhoo? Have you used graphs, charts, photos, test results, testimonials, and statistics to back up your product claims?

(i) **Have you included all necessary boilerplate copy?** Do you have all necessary information, such as effective and expiration dates of prices, how to order, notification of possible price changes, payment terms and methods, shipping and handling information, returns policy, quantity discounts, credit terms, sales tax, trademark information, copyright line, disclaimers, guarantees, warranties, limits of vendor liability.

(j) **Is it easy to place an order?** Does your copy explain how to order? Is there an order form? Is the order form easy to fill out? Is there enough space to write in the required information? Is a business reply envelope enclosed or attached to the order form? For a lead-generating catalogue, is a reply card, spec sheet, or other reply element included? Have you made clear to the reader what the next step is in the buying process? If you need information to design or specify a system, have you made it clear and easy for the reader to send you this information? If you want the reader to request more literature, have you described the literature and made it easy to send for these brochures?

If you think the words "easy" and "clear" have been overused in these guidelines, you're wrong. Everything you can do to make your message clearer and to make ordering a simple process will be reflected in your bottom line.

d. THE SELLING STARTS ON THE COVER

Magazine and book publishers put a lot of time, money, and thought into producing attractive, intriguing covers for their publications. They know that if a book or

134

magazine has a dull or uninteresting cover, readers won't pick it up and buy it.

It's the same with your catalogue. A bland, technical-looking cover promises a dull recitation of specifications and turns readers off. A cover with an enticing illustration and a strong selling message arouses curiosity and prods readers to open the catalogue. Here are a few suggestions for spicing up your catalogue cover:

(a) **Sell the product line.** A catalogue is really a "store in a mailbox." The more complete the store, the more likely customers will return to do all their shopping — again and again. A comprehensive product line is a big selling point. Why not stress it on the cover?

For example: Let's say you sell fasteners and have 3,200 product variations. Your catalogue shows only 1,250 models. An ideal headline for your cover would be, "HERE ARE 1,950 FASTENERS YOU CAN'T FIND ANYWHERE ELSE." Underneath would be a photo of the fasteners that you have and your competitors don't. Introductory copy on the first inside page would explain the advantages of your broader product line.

(b) **Sell solutions.** Sometimes, buyers aren't looking for specific products; they're looking for solutions to problems. You'll win them over if you show how your product solves the problem.

For example: The records administrator at a busy hospital has a problem organizing paper files, finding space to fit all the files, and pulling files quickly when a doctor needs them. This administrator is swamped with paper, but doesn't know what to do. Your microfilm storage systems are the ideal solution to this problem, but the records administrator isn't thinking of microfilm, so a cover with the ordinary headline "A Complete Line of Micrographic Equipment and Accessories" won't sell the product. A headline that *will* sell it is "HOW TO REDUCE A MOUNTAIN OF PAPER FILES TO A NEAT STACK OF MICROFICHE . . . AND FIND ANY FILE IN AS LITTLE AS 15 SECONDS." This headline sells a solution, not a product.

(c) **Sell service.** Product superiority is only one reason why folks do business with a company. There are many other factors: price, convenience, toll-free number, credit availability, trust, reputation, fast delivery, friendly salespeople, guarantee, service, and maintenance. You can generate interest in your catalogue by selling these services and intangibles — rather than the products — on the cover.

For example, stress service and maintenance. This can be as important as the quality of the product itself. Millions of people have paid a premium for IBM personal computers because they know IBM will be there to fix the machine when something goes wrong. Stressing your guarantee is another way of selling service commitment.

Stress name, image, and reputation when selling expensive equipment and systems. Buyers want to know that you have the resources to support your system for years to come and that you'll be around at least as long as the product lasts.

(d) **Start the catalogue on the cover.** Instead of using the cover as a mere pictorial introduction, or even a sales message, you can start your catalogue copy right on the cover. This is an effective way to draw the reader inside the book. Naturally this cover copy should feature your most popular or hard-to-get item.

Quill and other office supply catalogues do this (you can get a copy of the Quill catalogue by calling 1-800-789-1331).

(e) **Add a wrapper.** Wrappers are used to shout a sales message. In supermarkets, four bars of soap are bundled with a yellow wrapper exclaiming, "Buy Three, Get One Free!"

This technique is even working its way into bookstores: Stephen Fox's new book on the history of advertising, *The Mirror Makers*, was wrapped with a banner on which David Ogilvy and Rosser Reeves sang its praises. The same technique can be applied to catalogue covers. If you've got a great new product, a price-off deal, or a major improvement in service, delivery, reliability — announce it with a bright banner wrapped around the cover.

e. TEN WAYS TO MAKE YOUR CATALOGUE PULL MORE ORDERS

Sensible organization, crisp photography, bold graphics, and powerful copywriting are the keys to a successful catalogue. But experienced catalogue marketers also use dozens of sales-boosting gimmicks that have little to do with the basics of salesmanship or good copywriting. All we know is that these tricks of the trade work — and that's reason enough to use them. Here are ten that may be helpful to you:

(a) **Include a letter.** Nothing builds personality into a dry-as-dust catalogue as effectively as a warm, friendly, "personal" letter from the company president. If getting people to warm up to you is a problem — and it might be with new customers or with customers who have been disappointed by your products in the past — you can address customers directly with a letter. The letter can be printed on the cover or the inside front cover or printed on letterhead and bound into the catalogue. You can use this type of letter to introduce the catalogue, explain your ordering system, state a company philosophy, stress your dedication to service and quality, or alert the reader to new, discounted, and other special offerings. Whatever your message, adding a letter to a catalogue almost always increases sales.

(b) **Bursts.** Often used by cereal-makers to alert children to the prize inside the box, the burst (a star-shaped graphic with a copy line inside) can also draw a reader to special items

136

within a catalogue. Bursts can be used to highlight "price-off" deals, free trials, guarantees, and quantity discounts. Be careful to use bursts and other special graphic techniques (such as underlining, colored or boldface type, fake handwriting) sparingly. Overuse dilutes their effect.

(c) **Last-minute specials.** Insert into your catalogue a separate sheet featuring items added to your product line or discounted at the last minute. Tell the customer you received notice of these additions or bargains just in time for mailing but too late to print in the catalogue. This insert generates additional sales because people like to be in on the latest developments.

(d) **Give how-to information and tips of a general nature.** By adding tips on maintenance, repair, troubleshooting, applications, and operation you can increase demand for — and readership of — your catalogue. Including this useful information will also encourage buyers to keep your catalogue. The longer they have it, the more often they'll order from it. For instance, a hardware catalogue might include an article or table titled, "A Guide to Screw Selection." A filtration catalogue could include tips on "How to Clean and Care for Filters." Thomson's 83-page catalogue of ball bearings and shafts includes 17 pages on how to select, size, and install the equipment. If your information is exceptionally helpful, it can elevate your catalogue to the status of a reference work. Customers will keep it on their shelves for years.

(e) **Put your catalogue in a three-ring binder.** Expensive, but people won't throw out a hardback binder as readily as they would an ordinary paperback catalogue. Your customer also is more likely to keep your binder on the shelf because it's too bulky for the filing cabinet. This strategy is recommended only for catalogues aimed at purchasing agents and other corporate buyers.

(f) **Include product samples.** Sending your customers product samples gives you two advantages. First, mailings that have three-dimensional objects inside are more likely to be opened than flat envelopes. Second, engineers and other technical buyers often like to play with product samples, keeping them handy on their desks or shelves. A fine example of this technique is a brochure sent out for Gore-Tex, a sealant that prevents leaks in pipe sections when they are bolted together. The sample sealant was stuck to a photo of a pipe flange in the exact position it would be used in real life. The copy told the reader to remove the sample and put it through a series of simple tests (accomplished in five minutes at the reader's desk) to demonstrate its effectiveness.

(g) **List your customers.** Include a list of some of the firms that have bought from you, whether you have 300 or 3,000 names. Seeing such a list in print makes a powerful impression on your customers. They'll think, "How can I go wrong buying from these guys? Everybody in the world does business with them."

(h) **Include an order form.** Make it easy to fill out. Leave enough space for customers to write in necessary information. Bind it into the catalogue so it won't be lost or misplaced. (If your products can't be ordered by mail, include a spec sheet. The spec sheet asks prospects to provide key information on their applications — e.g., size of plant, hours of operation, type of process, and so on. With this information in hand, you can specify the equipment they need and tell them what it will cost.)

(i) **Include a business reply envelope (BRE).** The BRE is a self-addressed, postage-paid envelope the prospect can use to mail the order form or spec sheet back to you. Practically every consumer catalogue has a BRE. Most business catalogues don't. Business-to-business marketers think, "My prospects work in offices; they have a supply of envelopes and a postage meter handy. They don't care about the cost of postage, and their secretaries can take care of addressing the envelope." This may be true, but a BRE still boosts the response rate in business catalogues. Why? Not because they save the buyer the cost of postage, but because they make readers notice you'd like them to respond to your catalogue.

(j) **Make your catalogue an event.** Your buyers get a lot of catalogues in the mail, so the boredom factor is high. Anything you can do to make your catalogue mailing special, to stand out from the crowd, will boost sales and inquiries. One manufacturer sent a pound of chili powder with each catalogue, along with a cover letter proclaiming it "The Hottest Catalogue in the Office Supplies Industry." With a little imagination, you'll come up with an approach that fits your catalogue and your customers.

f. YOUR NEXT GREAT CATALOGUE IDEA IS IN YOUR MAILBOX

Catalogue marketers pay consultants and ad agencies thousands of dollars for marketing ideas. But you can get dozens of new ideas, FREE ideas, by studying catalogues produced by other firms.

Getting these catalogues is easy. First, get hold of a stack of magazines. Next, request any free catalogues the advertisers offer in their ads. Before you know it, your mailbox will be crammed with all sorts of catalogues, each containing a storehouse of great concepts you can use in your own marketing.

Following is a sampling of the kinds of techniques and tips you will find in catalogues you could receive this month.

(a) **Use product photos that demonstrate the product.** When people might be skeptical, use your catalogue to provide a product demonstration in print. Take computer paper, for example. It can be hard to tear off the perforated edges and sometimes the printed document rips in the process. In its computer supplies catalogue, Moore pictures a pair of hands pulling the perforated strips off Moore's paper easily and cleanly. Kudos to Moore — not many others have thought of a way to demonstrate a piece of paper in a photo.

(b) **Add value to the product.** Nixdorf Computer's "Solutionware" software catalogue offers many of the same computer programs as other catalogues. The difference? Nixdorf has created a list of seven powerful "extras" you get when ordering from the Solutionware catalogue. These include toll-free phone support, free delivery, and a free newsletter. This list of goodies appears at the beginning of the book and is repeated on the order form. Readers know they get more for their money when they buy their programs through Solutionware instead of another catalogue or a computer store.

(c) **Help the reader shop.** Compatibility is a big problem when selling computers and computer-related equipment and supplies. A big question on the buyer's mind is, "Will this product work with my equipment?" In an otherwise ordinary computer supply catalogue, Transnet gives its readers a bonus with a two-page "diskette compatibility chart." The chart lists the major brands and models of microcomputers alphabetically, along with the specific make of floppy disk designed for each machine. Uncertainty and confusion are eliminated. The buyer can place an order with confidence.

(d) **Show the results of using the product, not just the product itself.** Day-Timers' recent catalogue of calendars, pocket diaries, and appointment books is, as expected, illustrated with product photos. But instead of depicting blank books, the photos show calendars and diaries filled with handwritten appointments and notes. This adds realism and believability to the catalogue. It also shows how the calendar or diary could help organize the reader's life and schedule.

(e) **Turn your catalogue into a shopping system.** A catalogue is more than a book of product descriptions; it's a one-stop shopping center for your complete product line. For this reason, ease of use should be a major consideration in the conceptual phase of catalogue design. In the IBM cabling system catalogue, the first two sections of copy are "How to Use This Catalogue" and "How to Order." No introduction, no letter from the president, no product description — just simple, straightforward instructions on how to shop with the catalogue. Another nice touch is that the price list is printed opposite the order form, so the buyer doesn't have to search through the catalogue to find prices for the items being ordered.

If you make your catalogue interesting and easy to use, you'll find the orders pouring in.

14

KEEPING RECORDS AND IMPROVING YOUR RESULTS

Big consumer mailers test all the time. Publishers Clearinghouse tests just about everything . . . even (I hear) the slant of the indicia (the postal markings) on the outer envelope.

Companies that do not test and do not measure results are doomed to repeat their failures. They have no idea what works in direct mail — and what doesn't work. This is a mistake. In direct mail, you should not assume you know what will work. You should test to find out.

For example, copywriter Milt Pierce wrote a subscription package for *Good Housekeeping* magazine. His mailing became the "control" package for 25 years. That is, no package tested against it brought back as many subscriptions.

The envelope teaser and theme of that successful mailing was "32 Ways to Save Time and Money." Yet Milt Pierce says that when he applied the same theme to subscription mailings for other magazines — *Science Digest, Popular Mechanics, House Beautiful* — it failed miserably.

"There are no answers in direct mail except test answers," Eugene Schwartz writes in his book *Breakthrough Advertising*. "You don't know whether something will work until you test it. And you cannot predict test results based on past experience."

Even small increases in response rates can mean the difference between mediocre results and handsome profits. To get these increases, you must continually refine and improve your mail order marketing efforts. Why? Because if a test outperforms the existing ad or mailing (known in mail order marketing as the "control"), you will make more money every time you run the ad or mail the package.

My rule of thumb is this: watch what the major players in mail order do, then do the same thing. You can't do as much testing as they do, simply because they have more money and other resources. But you can learn from them and test more things more often. This is the road to mail order success.

a. TRACKING RESULTS

To do any kind of testing, you must have systems in place to measure the results of your mail order promotions and keep a record of those results.

On the simplest level, measuring results means counting the returned order coupons and checks you get each day (see Worksheet #1 and Sample #2 in chapter 7).

If you "key code" each ad or mailing, you will be able to tell where each inquiry or order came from. For instance, if your ad runs in the October issue of *Opportunity* magazine, your key code could be something like "OM-10." The OM is for *Opportunity* magazine and the 10 is for the date (October, the tenth month).

The key code is incorporated into your return address in the ad or on the order coupon as a department number. In this case, you would add Dept. OM-10 to your address.

When you do direct mail to rented mailing lists, you can have the mailing-list broker key code the labels for you. The cost is nominal; most brokers charge $1 per thousand labels to add key codes. When the labels are printed on the computer, the broker has the computer insert a code on each label to identify which list that label came from. If, rather than sticking the label on the outside of the envelope, you affix it to the reply card and then insert the reply card so it shows through the window on an envelope, you will receive the label back with the reply card and will be able to tell which list the order came from.

With key codes, you can count the response from each promotion so you know which promotions generated the best results.

You then must keep a record of how your promotions do, so when you test two different promotions you can compare them. Which generated the most inquiries? Which generated the most orders? Which was the most profitable?

Sometimes the promotion that generates the most orders or inquiries is not the most profitable promotion. If you run an ad in magazine A for $200 and it generates 200 inquiries, your cost is $1 per inquiry.

Let's say you run the same classified ad in magazine B, where it costs $50 and generates 100 inquiries. Although ad A generated more inquiries, ad B generated inquiries at a lower cost — 50¢ per inquiry — half of what ad A cost. From a profit standpoint, ad B is paying off better.

Appendix 3 lists mail order software packages you can use to track your mail order results.

b. BASICS OF TESTING

Here are the fundamental rules of testing:

(a) **You can test only one factor or variable at a time.** If you are doing a price test of $10 versus $20, you must use identical ad copy and layout except for the price difference. If you vary more than one factor at a time, and the response to the two ads is different, you will not know which factor caused the difference.

(b) **You must mail to at least 2,000 addresses.** To get a statistically valid test response to a direct mail package, you must mail at least 2,000 pieces to a portion of each mailing list you are testing. If you are testing two mailing lists, that means a test mailing of 4,000 pieces split evenly between the two lists.

(c) **You must keep track of responses and key code all tests.** If you are testing two postcards, key code the first "Dept. A" and the second "Dept. B." If you do not key code, you will not be able to measure the results of the test, and doing it will have been a waste of time.

(d) **Test as much as you can.** The more testing you do, the better your chances of generating a significant increase in response. Some of the factors you can test in mail order ads and direct mail include:

- Business reply mail versus "place stamp here"
- Business reply postcard versus fax-back form
- Color
- Copy
- Design
- Envelope size
- First class versus third class
- Format
- Guarantees
- Headlines
- Mailing lists
- Media
- Offer
- Outer envelope teasers
- Payment plans and options
- Premiums
- Price
- Product
- Themes or sales appeals
- Toll-free numbers versus long distance numbers

The three most important factors to test are mailing lists, prices, and offers.

c. WHAT QUESTIONS WILL TESTING ANSWER?

In your mail order business, you will be asking yourself many questions about what approach would work best. While you can theorize all you want to, the only way to get a definitive answer is to test.

"What price is best for my product?" You don't know. The low price is not always the most profitable and doesn't even always generate the most orders. If you are selling an audiocassette album presenting business information, and you are thinking of charging $59, you should also test $49 and $69. If the $49 price point generates the most responses, test $49 versus $39. If $49 wins that test, it is probably the best price. If $69 is the winner, test $69 versus $79. Your customers will tell you how much they will pay.

"What headline is best for my ad or mailing?" You don't know. If you think it should be "Easy to Operate," but your partner thinks the main benefit is "Uses Less Energy," test two ads or two mailings with these two different headlines and themes. Again, your customers will tell you whether ease of operation or energy conservation is most important to them.

If you are doing a mailing, you might say to yourself, "Why spend the money on a full-blown direct mail package? Why not go with an inexpensive trifold mailer?" My advice? Test 2,000 of each format. While the self-mailer costs less, it may not necessarily be the most profitable package. Testing formats — a package versus a trifold mailer or a self-mailer versus a single postcard — makes sense. You don't know which will work for you until you test it.

It's especially important in direct mail to test mailing lists. The best mailing list for your offer may pull five to ten times the response of a poor list. In addition, you cannot tell which lists will be the winner until you test. Therefore, the more lists you test, the better your chances of finding one or more winning lists. It's better to test smaller quantities per list (1,500 to 2,000 names each) and get more lists in your test mailing than to test a lot of names per list (5,000 is typical) and test fewer lists.

Test offers. This means not only the price but the offer as a whole. Will you increase response by giving a premium, or free gift, with every order? What about giving two premiums with the order? Should you charge a flat price of $22 or present the price as $19 plus $3 for shipping and handling?

Changing the offer can increase the response twofold or more. Not every offer test makes such a dramatic difference, and many tests turn out to show no difference in response whatsoever. But then you do a test of a particular offer and your response soars.

Most direct mail questions can be answered with a test. These include:

- "Should I use a plain outer envelope or put a teaser on it?"

- "Should I mail first class or third class?"

- "Should we use business reply envelopes or require the customer to affix postage to a plain, pre-addressed envelope?"

Mail order experts tell their clients, "You must have a guarantee." Perhaps your reaction is, "I don't want to offer a guarantee because everybody will take advantage of me, order my product, use it, copy it, and then return it." Experienced mail order operators know that a strong guarantee lifts response and, for a decent product, results in few returns. But don't take their word for it. Test it for yourself.

"Every time you do a mailing you should test something," says mail order entrepreneur James Lumley. "If you don't, you've wasted an opportunity to learn something about the prospects who respond to your offer."

15

MAKING MONEY FROM YOUR CUSTOMER LIST

Your customer names are worth money, both to you and others. If you maintain your list, you will be able to increase your sales to your own customer list *and* rent the list for a profit to others.

a. MAINTAIN YOUR CUSTOMER LIST ON YOUR COMPUTER

You can use any kind of data base program to keep your customer files on your computer. Or you can buy one of the specialized mail order programs listed in Appendix 3. Be sure to capture the following information:

- Name
- Address
- City, state or province, zip or postal code
- Phone number, fax number, e-mail address (if available)
- Items ordered
- Amount of money spent per order
- Dates of purchases

As we noted in chapter 4, it is much less expensive, and therefore much more profitable, to sell more to existing customers — the buyers on your customer list — than to sell a product to a new customer for the first time. Therefore, it's a good idea to send regular mailings — at least quarterly — to your customer list. These mailings could be sales letters, direct mail packages, catalogues, or mini-catalogues.

In your promotion, recognize the recipients as valued customers of your firm. Tell how you have selected products you know they will enjoy and find useful. If you offer discounts, let them know they are getting these specials because they are good customers.

These regular mailings are also useful for keeping your list up-to-date, as any undeliverable mail will be returned to you. You can take dead addresses off the list and save the costs of mailing to them in the future.

b. MAKE MONEY BY RENTING YOUR LIST

A well-managed list can generate $1 to $3 or more per name each year in revenue from rentals to other mail order entrepreneurs. If you have a house list of 50,000 names, this means you can make an additional $50,000 to $150,000 or more in income with virtually no extra work or involvement on your part. It's a sweet deal!

You will have acquired many of the names on your house list after prospects responded to a mailing you sent out to a list rented from other list owners. Those list owners have made money renting you their names; why not make money renting those names back to them?

1. How list rental works

Mailing lists rent from $75 to $150 or more per thousand names. As the list owner, you receive this amount minus a 20% commission fee that goes to the list manager.

A mailing list manager is an individual or firm that markets your house mailing list of customers and prospects on the open market. The list manager promotes your list to mailers, agencies, list brokers, consultants, and others looking to rent mailing lists. A list manager represents one or more specific lists and gets a management fee every time the list is rented. A list broker, by comparison, arranges rental of any list the customer wants and gets a commission when recommended lists are rented.

If you have a house list of customers and prospects that you are currently renting to other marketers, a professional list manager can reduce the administrative work of list management while increasing your list rental revenues.

If you don't currently rent your house list but are thinking of doing so, a list manager can help you evaluate the list's marketability and profit potential and can then market and promote your list to generate additional income.

List managers are usually not interested in managing a list of less than 10,000 names. They may make an exception, however, if your list is unique or highly specialized.

Although list managers prefer that your list be computerized, it's not mandatory. If your list is not in computer format, the list management company can key and convert it for you — you won't need to do it yourself. You can send your names on tape, disk, index cards, reader service inquiry reports, even scraps of paper. The list management company can scan, key in, or do whatever it takes to convert the list to computer files for you.

The list manager makes money only if and when the list is rented. All expenses, including those involving computer systems and promotion, are paid by the list manager, not the list owner. The list manager's compensation is a 20% commission on the income generated from rental of the list.

Pick up any issue of *Direct Marketing, DM News, Target Marketing,* or one of the other direct mail magazines listed in Appendix 2. Each of these magazines will have a section announcing "new lists available." The names and phone numbers of the list management companies that manage these lists will appear in the blurb. Call them to discuss the possibility of their managing your list.

By the way, in the example given above, not marketing your 50,000-name list means you leave an extra $50,000 to $100,000 in profit on the table every year. Also, since 20% of the people on your list move every year, once they're gone you lose that income unless you rent those names now. And that points out an additional benefit of renting your list. Renters return undeliverable mail to you, so you are able to update your mailing list with your list renters paying the cost of the postage!

2. What to do if a customer complains

Some people do not like getting direct mail. Others may like to order products from catalogues and mail packages you send them but do not want you to rent out their name to other mail order marketers.

If customers say "Don't rent my name," you can always set up your data base so that these names are not printed when you rent your list to others.

The Direct Marketing Association in New York (see Appendix 5) also maintains a data base of consumers who do not want to have their names rented out. You can encourage your buyers to contact the DMA if they are concerned.

APPENDIX 1
BOOKS AND AUDIOCASSETTES
ON DIRECT MAIL AND ADVERTISING

There are dozens of books on mail order, direct mail, and advertising. Read as many as you can. The only way to learn this business is by experience — either yours or someone else's. Learning by doing is effective but costly. Read about the experience of others first so you can avoid their costly mistakes and model your promotions on their winners.

Business-to-Business Direct Marketing by Tracy Emerick and Bernie Goldberg (North Hampton, NH: Direct Marketing Publishers). Solid information on business-to-business direct marketing. Especially strong on planning, strategy, data bases, catalogues, and telemarketing.

The Business-to-Business Direct Marketing Handbook by Roy G. Ljungren (New York: AMACOM). A thorough and comprehensive book on all aspects of business-to-business direct marketing.

The Complete Guide to Marketing and the Law by Robert J. Posch, Jr. (Englewood Cliffs, NJ: Prentice Hall). Perhaps the most comprehensive layperson's guide ever written on marketing law.

The Copywriter's Handbook: A Step-by-Step Guide to Writing Copy That Sells by Robert W. Bly (New York: Henry Holt & Co.). How to write effective copy for ads, direct mail, and other promotions.

How to Make a Whole Lot More than $1,000,000 Writing, Commissioning, Publishing, and Selling 'How-To' Information Products by Dr. Jeffrey Lant (Cambridge, MA: JLA Publications). One of the top "how to write and sell information products by mail" books. Extremely detailed, often innovative.

How to Publish a Book and Sell a Million Copies by Ted Nicholas (Indian Shores, FL: Nicholas Direct). One of the great mail order entrepreneurs of all time shows how to make money selling books and other information products by mail.

How to Start and Operate a Mail Order Business by Julian L. Simon (New York: McGraw-Hill). Comprehensive guide to the mail order business, aimed at the novice, but encyclopedic in coverage.

Infomercial Writers Market Guide by Jay Winchester (Sudbury, MA: Blue Dolphin Communications). How to write effective infomercials.

Mail Order by Melvin Powers (Los Angeles, CA: Wilshire Publishing Company). A super-successful mail order entrepreneur reveals his secrets.

Mail Order! by Eugene Schwartz (New York, NY: Boardroom Books). A how-to-do-it book by perhaps the most successful mail order copywriter and practitioner.

Mail Order Laws by Kalvin Kahn (Philadelphia, PA: Redwood House). Plain-English guide to the most important laws affecting mail order marketers.

Mail Order Success Secrets by Bob Kalian (Yonkers, NY: Roblin Press). Charmingly written account of one man's success in mail order and his advice for your own mail order ventures.

Money Making Marketing by Dr. Jeffrey Lant (Cambridge, MA: JLA Publications). Superior how-to book on marketing, with an emphasis on direct marketing.

Power-Packed Direct Mail by Robert W. Bly (New York: Henry Holt & Co.). A layperson's guide to creating effective direct mail.

Tough Selling For Tough Times by Murray Raphel and Neil Raphel (Atlantic City, NJ: Raphel Publishing). Good information on general selling plus some specifics on mail order selling.

Twenty-Two Secrets of Professional Direct Mail Copywriters by David Yale (Bayside, NY: Yale Info, Inc.), audiocassette. How to write direct mail copy that sells, as told by a top practitioner.

U.S. Direct Marketing Law: The Complete Handbook for Managers by Richard J. Leighton and Alfred S. Regnery (Washington, DC: Regnery Gateway). Excellent reference book on direct marketing law.

Writer's Utopia Formula Report by Jerry Major Buchanan (Vancouver, WA: Towers Club USA). A solid course on the basics of selling reports, booklets, and other information products by mail, especially through classified ads.

Writing for Fun and Money: How to Make Money Writing and Selling Simple Information by Joe Barnes (Fort Ann, NY: Barnes Books). The printing and production technology described here is dated, but the strong presentation on the fundamentals of mail order selling is still right on target.

APPENDIX 2
DIRECT MARKETING PERIODICALS

The following magazines and newsletters, which cover all of North America, are packed with good how-to information on direct marketing techniques, as well as news of new lists, formats, and other resources. Many are available free or at a nominal cost.

Business Marketing Magazine
740 North Rush Street
Chicago, IL 60611
Phone: (312) 649-5260

Monthly magazine devoted exclusively to business-to-business marketing.

Direct
Cowles Business Media
6 River Bend Center
P.O. Box 4949
Stamford, CT 06907-0949
Phone: (203) 358-9900

One of several monthly magazines covering the direct marketing industry. Free to those in the business. Mixes news, analysis, case histories, and how-to.

Direct Marketing Magazine
Hoke Communications
224 Seventh Street
Garden City, NY 11530
Phone: (516) 746-6700

A monthly magazine covering the direct marketing industry. Many how-to articles.

The Direct Response Specialist
Galen Stilson
Stilson & Stilson
P.O. Box 1075
Tarpon Springs, FL 34688
Phone: (813) 786-1411

Monthly newsletter on selling via direct response advertising and direct mail. Good how-tos on the basics of direct marketing.

DM News
Mill Hollow
19 W. 21st Street
New York, NY 10010
Phone: (212) 741-2095

Weekly newspaper covering the direct marketing industry. Free to those in the business.

Information Marketing Report
P.O. Box 2038
Vancouver, WA 98668
Phone: (360) 574-3084

Monthly newsletter on how to sell information by mail. Highly recommended.

Money Making Opportunities
Success Publishing International
11071 Ventura Boulevard
Studio City, CA 91604
Phone: (818) 980-9166

One of the better business opportunity magazines.

Sure-Fire Business Success Catalog
Dr. Jeffrey Lant
JLA Publications
50 Follen Street, Suite 507
Cambridge, MA 02139
Phone: (617) 547-6372

Quarterly 16-page catalogue containing more than 120 recommendations on small business marketing and management. Call or write for free one-year subscription.

Target Marketing Magazine
North American Publishing Co.
401 N. Broad Street
Philadelphia, PA 19108
Phone: (215) 238-5300

Monthly magazine covering the direct marketing industry. Concise, quick-reading format. Free to those in the industry.

Who's Mailing What? and The Direct Marketing Archive
Dennison Hatch
P.O. Box 8180
Stamford, CT 06905
Phone: (203) 329-2666

Unique monthly newsletter analyzing winning direct mail packages (mostly large-volume consumer mailings). Subscribers gain free access to the Direct Marketing Archive, a large collection of sample direct mail packages organized by category.

APPENDIX 3
SOFTWARE FOR MAIL ORDER BUSINESSES

In addition to keeping paper files, you should keep your records on a computer. Many specialized software programs are available for mail order businesses. Here is a partial list (these companies operate throughout North America).

FastTrack
Fastech and Gelco Information Network
400 Parkway Drive
Broomall, PA 19008
Phone: (610) 359-9200

LPS
Simplified Office Systems
16025 Van Aken Boulevard, Suite 102
Cleveland, OH 44120
Phone: (216) 572-1050

MailEasy
Applied Information Group
720 King Georges Road
Fords, NJ 08863
Phone: (908) 738-8444

Mail Order Manager (MOM)
Dydacomp Development Corporation
150 River Road, Suite N-1
Montville, NJ 07045
Phone: (201) 335-1256

Marketing Professional's InfoCenter/Smart Marketing Suite
Group One Software
4200 Parliament Place, Suite 600
Lanham, MD 20706
Phone: (301) 918-0721

MSM
Marketing Information Services
1840 Oak Avenue
Suite 400
Evanston, IL 60201
Phone: (847) 491-0682

Order Power!
Computer Solutions, Inc.
6187 NW 167th Street, Unit H33
Miami, FL 33015
Phone: (305) 558-7000

Pro-Mail
Software Marketing Associates
2080 Silas Deane Highway
Rocky Hill, CT 06067-2341
Phone: (860) 721-8929

ProSmart
Digital Arts LLC
1551 Valley Forge Road, Suite 259
Lansdale, PA 19446-5459
Phone: (215) 361-2650

APPENDIX 4
MAILING LIST BROKERS

There are numerous firms renting mailing lists and data bases. Here are some of the best. This list is by no means exhaustive, and there are many additional reputable firms not listed here. See also your local Yellow Pages under "mailing lists" or "direct mail."

American List Council
Phone: (908) 874-4300

Compilers Plus
Phone: 1-800-431-2914

Cornerstone List Brokers
Phone: (416) 932-9555

Database America
Phone: (201) 476-2000

Direct Media
Phone: (203) 532-1000

Edith Roman Associates
Phone: 1-800-223-2194

Hugo Dunhill
Phone: 1-800-811-6013

PCS
Phone: 1-800-532-5478

WorldData
Phone: 1-800-331-8102

APPENDIX 5
DIRECT MARKETING ORGANIZATIONS

The following organizations provide information and support to their members, most of whom are direct marketers or direct marketing service firms, such as ad agencies and list brokers.

DMA Direct Marketing Association, Inc.
11 West 42nd Street
New York, NY 10036-8096
Phone: (212) 768-7277

A national association for direct marketers.

Newsletter Publishers Association
Phone: (703) 527-2333

Professional organization for publishers of subscription newsletters.

In Canada:

Canadian Direct Marketing Association
1 Concord Gate, #607
Don Mills, ON M3C 3N6
Phone: (416) 391-2362

You might also consider joining one or more of the many local or regional direct marketing clubs. To find out whether there is such a group in your area, ask colleagues, consult the national marketing association, or check meeting announcements in *Direct Marketing* magazine (see Appendix 2).

APPENDIX 6
PRODUCT SOURCES

If you do not make a product, you can buy products at wholesale discounts and resell them via mail order at retail prices. The following companies are possible product sources. Many of them ship within North America.

Brandel Communications Inc.
1859 N. Pine Island Road
Plantation, FL 33322
Phone: (954) 462-8692

How-to reports and guides suitable for mail order sale.

Kaeser & Blair, Inc.
4236 Grissom Drive
Batavio, Ohio 45103
Phone: 1-800-642-9790

Ad specialities

Lakeside Products Co.
6646 N. Western Avenue
Chicago, IL 60645
Phone: 1-800-666-4404 or
(773) 761-5495

General merchandise

The Mellinger Co.
6100 Variel Avenue
Woodland Hills, CA 91367-3770
Phone: 1-800-213-3943

General merchandise

N.W.C.
158 Bloomingdale Street
Chelsea, MA 02159
Phone: (617) 381-7300

Consumer electronics (TVs, VCRs, computers, camcorders)

Specialty Merchandise Corporation (SMC)
9401 De Soto Avenue
Chatsworth, CA 91311
Phone: 1-800-345-4SMC

General merchandise

WorldWide Business Exchange
Philander Company
P.O. Box 5385
Cleveland, TN 37320-5385
Phone: (706) 259-2280

General merchandise

APPENDIX 7
ADVERTISING MEDIA

Here is a partial list of publications known to be good for mail order advertising. Complete information on all the publications — including address, phone number, circulation, and advertising rates — may be found in the publication *Standard Rate & Data Service*, which covers all of North America (published by Standard Rate & Data Service, 1700 Higgins Road, Des Plaines, IL 60018-5605; Phone: (847) 375-5000).

American Legion

Better Homes and Gardens

Black Enterprise

Canadian Gardening

Canadian Geographic

Canadian Seniority

Capper's Weekly

Changing Times

Crafts 'n Things

Elks Magazine

Entrepreneur

Family Circle

Field & Stream

Globe

Grit

In Business

Income Opportunities

Kiwanis Magazine

Los Angeles Times

Modern Maturity

Money-Making Opportunities

Mother Earth News

National Enquirer

The New Yorker

Opportunity

Organic Gardening

Outdoor Life

Parade Magazine

Popular Mechanics

Popular Science

Practical Homeowner

Saturday Evening Post

Spare Time

Spotlight

The Star

TV Guide

USA Today

Yankee

The following companies buy mail order space at a discount for clients. Using one of them may reduce your media bills.

Linick Media
7 Putter Lane
Middle Island, NY 11953
Phone: (516) 924-8555

Novus Marketing
601 Lakeshore Parkway, Suite 900
Minneapolis, MN 55305
Phone: (612) 476-7700

APPENDIX 8
SUPPLIER DIRECTORY

a. COPYWRITERS

The Copywriter's Council of America
7 Putter Lane
Middle Island, NY 11953
Phone: (516) 924-8555

Provides freelance copywriters tailored to the project and to the client's budget.

Steve Manning
2065 Blue Ridge Crescent
Pickering, ON L1X 2N5
Phone: (905) 686-4891

b. GRAPHIC ARTISTS

Stan Greenfield
39 W. 37th Street, 14th Floor
New York, NY 10018
Phone: (212) 889-0762 or (201) 902-9773

First-rate freelance graphic artist specializing in direct mail.

Lithart Associates, Inc.
43 Lesmill Road
Don Mills, ON M3B 2T8
Phone: (416) 391-4036

Rutledge & Brown Company
Steve Brown
25 West 39th Street, Suite 1101
New York, NY 10018
Phone: (212) 730-7959

Freelance graphic artist specializing in brochures and collateral; also does excellent work in direct mail. A lot of business-to-business experience.

c. LETTER SHOPS

Arrow Mailing
3780 Peter Street
Windsor, ON N9C 4H2
Phone: (519) 971-8155

Fala Direct Marketing
Mitch Hisiger
70 Marcus Drive
Melville, NY 11747
Phone: (516) 694-1919

Good full-service letter shop, especially for personalized mailings. Send for free booklet *Should I Personalize?*

Jerry Lake Mailing Service
620 Frelinghuysen Avenue
Newark, NJ 07714
Phone: (201) 565-9268

Good full-service letter shop. Reasonable prices, especially for smaller volume mailings.

Postal Promotions Ltd.
1100 Birchmont Road
Scarborough, ON M1K 5H9
Phone: (416) 752-8100

d. FULFILLMENT HOUSES

Direct Communications Marketing
1175 Grant Street
Vancouver, BC V6A 2J7
Phone: (604) 258-9300

Fala Direct Marketing
70 Marcus Drive
Melville, NY 11747
Phone: (516) 694-1919

INDAS
35 Rivieria Drive, Unit 17
Markham, ON L3R 8N4
Phone: (905) 946-0400

Mailco
150 South Main Street
Wood Ridge, NJ 07075
Phone: (201) 777-9500